DAVID SUZUKI
and Kathy Vanderlinden

From Dinosaur Breath to Pizza from Dirt

David Suzuki Foundation

GREYSTONE BOOKS

Douglas & McIntyre Publishing Group

Vancouver/Toronto/New York

Greystone Books
A division of Douglas & McIntyre Ltd.
2323 Quebec Street, Suite 201
Vancouver, British Columbia V5T 4S7

David Suzuki Foundation
219-2211 West 4th Avenue
Vancouver, British Columbia V6K 4S2

Originated by Greystone Books and published simultaneously in Australia by Allen & Unwin, Sydney.

Canadian Cataloguing in Publication Data

Suzuki, David, 1936–
  You are the earth

  Includes index.
  ISBN 1-55054-751-8

  I. Ecology—Juvenile literature. 2. Human ecology—Juvenile
literature. 3. Natural history—Juvenile literature. I. Vanderlinden,
Kathy. II. Title.
QH541.14.S899 1999   j577   C99-910621-X

Library of Congress Cataloging-in-Publication Data is available.

Editing by Nancy Flight
Text design and production by Randy McPhee, Eric Ansley & Associates Ltd.
Jacket design by Peter Cocking
Front jacket photograph by Chick Rice
Printed and bound in Hong Kong by C & C Offset Printing Co. Ltd.

Every attempt has been made to trace accurate ownership of copyrighted material in this book. Errors and
omissions will be corrected in subsequent editions, provided that notification is sent to the publisher.

The publisher gratefully acknowledges the support of the Canada Council for the Arts and of the British
Columbia Ministry of Tourism, Small Business and Culture. The publisher also acknowledges the financial
support of the Government of Canada through the Book Publishing Industry Development Program.
Canadä

Contents

Acknowledgments and Credits

The authors acknowledge the tremendous contribution of Amanda McConnell, who cowrote *The Sacred Balance,* on which this book is based. They also wish to thank David Barnum of West Sechelt Elementary School, Sechelt, B.C.; Gordon Li of Stoney Creek Community School, Burnaby, B.C.; and Susan Martin of Delta Resource Centre, Delta, B.C., for reviewing the manuscript and offering useful suggestions.

The authors are grateful to the following people for providing information and advice: Elliot M. Fratkin, Associate Professor of Anthropology, Smith College, Northampton, Mass.; Quentin Mackie, Assistant Professor of Anthropology, University of Victoria; Robert S. Schemenauer, Cloud Physicist, Atmospheric Environment Service, Environment Canada; Y.N. (Kenny) Kwok, Associate Professor of Physiology, University of British Columbia; and Peter Shin, Department of Nutritional Sciences, Faculty of Medicine, University of Toronto. Thanks go also to the members of ORCA, especially Kathleen Fawley, Tristan Huntington, David Meszaros, Les Meszaros, and Michael VanInsberghe; to Lauren Telford and Angela Reid of the Return of the Peregrine Falcon project; and to Craig Kielburger, founder of Free the Children, for their inspiring contributions to the book. Finally, we are indebted to our editor, Nancy Flight, for her collaboration, encouragement, unfailing good humor, and meticulous attention to the manuscript.

Credits

Statistics in "The Call of the Mall" are from the pamphlet "All Consuming Passion: Waking Up from the American Dream," 3rd ed. (Seattle: Northwest Environment Watch and New Road Map Foundation, 1998). Myths and legends were based on the following sources: "Out of the Sky" from Michael J. Caduto and Joseph Bruchac, *Keepers of the Earth: Native Stories and Environmental Activities for Children* (Saskatoon, SK: Fifth House Publishers, 1991); "The Animal Canoe" from "Tales of the Heroes" in Jan Knappert and Francesca Pelizzali, *Kings, Gods & Spirits from African Mythology* (Vancouver/Toronto: Douglas & McIntyre, 1986); "The Gift of the Spider Woman" from B.C. Sproul, *Primal Myths: Creating the World* (New York: Harper & Row, 1979); "Lifting Up the Sky" from "Pushing Up the Sky" in Richard Erdoes and Alfonso Ortiz, *American Indian Myths and Legends* (New York: Pantheon Books, 1984).

Commissioned Illustrations

Jeff Burgess: p. 17; p. 47; p. 48; p. 71; p. 97.
Lorne Carnes: pp. 34–35; p. 40; p. 64; pp. 86–87.
Kveta Jelinek/Three In a Box: p. 13; p. 14; p. 16; p. 28; pp. 32–33; p.44; p. 46; p. 56; p. 58; p. 59; p. 62; p. 63.
Tadeusz Majewski/Three In a Box: p. 20; p. 30; p. 49; p. 61; p. 68; p. 94; p. 106.
Rose Zgodzinski/Three In a Box: p. 10; p. 19; p. 27; p. 37; p. 45.

Photography

EyeWire: pp. 24–25; p. 72.
Craig Keilburger: p. 100; p. 103.
Images® copyright 1999 PhotoDisc, Inc.: p. 23; p. 26; p. 39; p. 51; p. 65; p. 72; p. 73; p. 74; p. 76; p. 79; p. 88; p. 93.
Dr. Robert Schemenauer: p. 38.
Ken L. Woodward: p. 104.

Preface

The very first thing I remember happened when I was about four years old. My dad was planning a camping trip and had taken me to a sporting goods store to buy a tent. He found a little pup tent he liked and set it up right on the floor of the store. Then we both crawled in and lay down together to make sure that there was enough room for both of us. The prospect of going camping was so exciting to me that I've never forgotten that moment. That camping trip was the beginning of my lifelong love of nature and of my dream that I would someday become a naturalist and travel to exotic places to collect animals.

When I grew up, I did become a scientist who studied nature. My work was filled with the wonder of discovery. Beetles had been my childhood passion, and now I spent much of my time studying another fascinating insect, the fruit fly. It amazed me that I could study parts of nature to my heart's content and get paid for doing it!

But in the 1960s I started hearing reports of dangers threatening the natural world. We humans were polluting the air, destroying lakes and rivers, killing off entire groups of animals and their habitats, and putting our whole environment—our home—at risk. Like many people at that time, I began working with others to get laws passed to protect the environment.

In the late 1970s, I found myself in the Queen Charlotte Islands off the north coast of British Columbia. The Haida people who have lived on these islands call them Haida Gwaii. For thousands of years the forests had provided shelter and food for the Haida people. But now the trees are also valuable as logs for the forest industry. So for years a struggle had been going on between the forest companies and the Haida about what to do with the trees.

While I was in Haida Gwaii, I met a Haida artist named Guujaaw. Since many loggers were Haida, and since forest companies brought money into the Haida community, I asked him why he was against the logging. Guujaaw's answer changed the way I looked at the world. He said, "If they cut down all the trees, of course we Haida will still be here. But then we'll be like everybody else."

I thought about his words for a long time. I realized he was saying that the Haida people don't think of trees as just part of their landscape—they are part of the people, too. Those islands—along with the salmon, cedars, ravens, ocean, mountains, and skies—have been home to the Haida since the beginning of memory. They make the Haida who they are. If the forests are cut down, a large part of what makes the Haida people special and different will be lost.

In the years since that conversation, I have met and worked with Native people around the world. I have been involved in projects with the Aborigines in Australia, the Ainu in Japan, the Kayapo and Yanomami of the Amazon, the Embara of Colombia, the Papua New Guineans, the Penan in Borneo, the San on the Kalahari Desert, and many First Nations people in Canada. And everywhere, even among the poorest groups, people say that they are connected to the land. Native people often say, "The Earth is our mother."

As a scientist, I have come to know that they are right. We are made of water, air, and the food we eat from the Earth's soil. I've come to realize—thanks to Guujaaw and many others since then—that it is a mistake to think of the environment as something "out there," separate from us. We *are* the Earth.

The problem with so many battles about the environment is that we get caught up in debates that force us to choose between two valuable things—spotted owls *or* jobs, logging *or* parks, people *or* wildlife. When problems are put that way, no matter what happens someone or something will lose. But if we care about a future for coming generations, we can't have any losers. We have to decide what is really important.

I wrote this book to show what we need to survive. We need clean air, water, and soil and the sun's energy to stay alive. And those four elements are provided by the wonderful variety of plant and animal life on this planet. We don't understand how it all works, but nature itself gives us the elements that all life depends on.

We need love to make us human. And we can best love and be loved when we have strong families, communities, and surrounding ecosystems. We also need to recognize that there are great mysteries in our lives we can never understand. We need to have sacred places, wildernesses we treasure because they feed our spirit.

These are the values that all people can agree on. The challenge is to create societies and ways of life based on those needs.

I hope that by reading this book you discover what you must do to meet all those needs, and that you learn some interesting things about yourself and the Earth. At the end of the book are questions to help you remember those things. You'll also find some great activities that tell you more about the wonders of air, water, soil and the sun.

Enjoy your discoveries. Open your eyes, mind and heart to the beauty of the world. Then you can help make it a better place for yourself and all the other children who will inherit it.

David Suzuki
Vancouver, British Columbia

Walking On Air

1

You probably don't think much about air. You can't see it or hear it or grab a handful of it. It's almost as if it weren't there. And yet it's just about the most precious thing in the world.

Try holding your breath for five minutes. Can you do it? Of course not. Your body won't let you. You can try to hold your breath until your face turns red and purple, but the muscles in your lungs and chest will soon force you to breathe. That's how much your body needs air.

From your first breath to your last, you must have air. If you didn't have air for just five or six minutes, you would die. All of us Earthlings—people, animals, and plants—need air to live. And the amazing thing is, not only does air keep us alive, it also ties us together. It's as if we were swimming in an "air soup." When you breathe out, atoms—tiny, invisible "bits"—of air fly out of your nose and go right up the noses of all the people near you!

You're Breathing Dinosaur Breath

Did you know that the next breath you take will contain dinosaur breath? It sounds weird, but it's true. Here's how it works. Air is really a mixture of several gases. A gas is a light, invisible substance that floats freely in the air—steam, for example. Two of these gases, nitrogen and oxygen, make up almost all of the air.

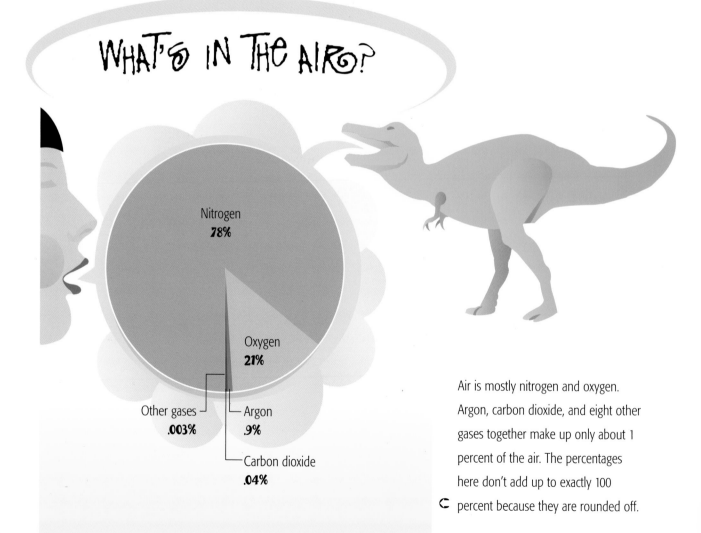

WHAT'S IN THE AIR?

Nitrogen
78%

Oxygen
21%

Other gases
.003%

Argon
.9%

Carbon dioxide
.04%

Air is mostly nitrogen and oxygen. Argon, carbon dioxide, and eight other gases together make up only about 1 percent of the air. The percentages here don't add up to exactly 100 percent because they are rounded off.

There's only a small amount of the gas argon in the air. Yet an American astronomer named Harlow Shapley calculated that each breath you breathe out, or exhale, contains about 30,000,000,000,000,000,000 (let's call it 30 zillion) atoms of argon. (That's the kind of thing scientists like to figure out.)

In a few minutes, those atoms you've exhaled will travel right through your neighborhood. In a year, they will have spread all around the Earth, and about 15 of them will be right back where they started—in your nose. Argon is always in you and around you. And not just in you but also in your best friend, your favorite pop star, the birds, snakes, flowers, trees, and worms. All of us air breathers are sharing those same argon atoms.

So here's where the dinosaur part comes in. An interesting thing about argon atoms is that they never change or die—they stay around forever. That means that thousands of years ago, an Egyptian slave building the pyramids breathed some of the same argon atoms that later Joan of Arc, Napoleon, and his horse breathed. And some of those were argon atoms exhaled by dinosaurs that lived 70 million years ago. They all breathed out argon atoms into the atmosphere—ready for you to breathe in as you read this sentence. And when you exhale your next 30 zillion argon atoms, some of them will one day find their way into the noses of babies not even born yet.

What's true of argon is true of air in general. Air joins together all of Earth's creatures—past, present, and future.

Take a *Deep* Breath . . .

Imagine Shaquille O'Neal pounding down the court, dribbling the ball at top speed. Pretty impressive show, especially when you realize he's also filtering the air with his lungs. Each minute, he's taking 40 to 60 breaths and he's pumping 2 to 4 liters (quarts) of air through his lungs.

Your body has a wonderful system for getting air into every part of your body and making sure it's as pure as possible when it gets there. Even when you're just hanging out, not running and jumping like Shaq, you take about 10 breaths a minute, or 600 an hour.

Imagine what happens when you take one breath. Air enters your nose and gets filtered by tiny hairs lining the inside. They trap large dust particles and other bits that shouldn't get into your lungs. These bits will be expelled when you sneeze or blow your nose.

As the air rushes along the nasal chamber, getting warmed and moistened, it passes the olfactory bulb. This area sends messages to the brain about the odor of the air coming in. You're not as good at smelling as a dog is (it can tell one person from another by smell), but you're pretty good. You can tell if there are roses in the room, if dinner's burning on the stove, or if someone's wearing running shoes without socks.

Next the air rushes down your windpipe and into the bronchi, or branches, of your lungs. Bronchi are tubes that split into smaller tubes called bronchioles, which keep branching out. At the very ends of the smallest bronchi are air sacs, like tiny grapes. You have about 300 million of these air sacs in your lungs. If they were flattened out, they could cover the area of Shaquille O'Neal's basketball court!

When the air gets to the sacs, it passes through their walls into your blood vessels. Air has now become part of your body, ready to go to work for you. The oxygen in the air is the most important gas—the one you must have to live. Every tissue and organ,

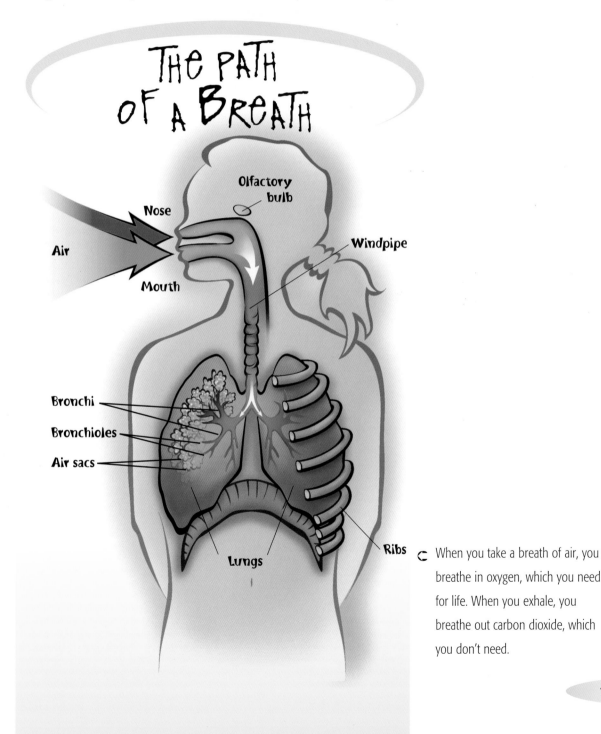

THE PATH OF A BREATH

Olfactory bulb

Nose

Air

Windpipe

Mouth

Bronchi

Bronchioles

Air sacs

Lungs

Ribs

When you take a breath of air, you breathe in oxygen, which you need for life. When you exhale, you breathe out carbon dioxide, which you don't need.

YOUR AIR SACS CLOSE UP

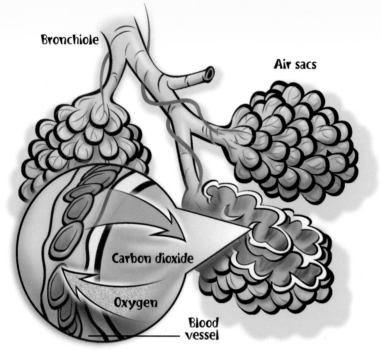

Bronchiole

Air sacs

Carbon dioxide

Oxygen

Blood vessel

⊂ Oxygen moves from the air sacs into the surrounding blood vessels. Carbon dioxide, which is made in the body, moves the opposite way—from the blood vessels into the air sacs. From there it is breathed out.

especially your heart and brain, needs a constant supply of oxygen to do its job. So oxygen is carried in your bloodstream throughout your body.

While all this is going on, the gas carbon dioxide is being formed as a waste product of body processes such as digestion. Your body doesn't need carbon dioxide, so it gets rid of most of it. Carbon dioxide travels the same route as oxygen only backwards—from your blood to your lungs to your nose, where you exhale it into the outside air. And it all happens automatically. You don't have to think about it, because your body breathes for you, even when you're asleep.

Air is always part of you. And the air you exhale becomes part of everyone nearby, too. If air were visible, you would see how it connects us all.

How Air Got to Be Perfect

Earth's air has exactly the right mixture of gases you need to live. How do you think this perfect arrangement came to be? Let's imagine we could board a timeship and go back about 2.5 billion years, as life was beginning to take hold on Earth.

Stepping out of the timeship, we look around. We see a landscape of rock and murky water, with no trees or plants or even soil anywhere. But we don't have time to explore, because in two minutes we're dead! Why? Because the air has almost no oxygen in it. Not only that, we're roasted because the temperature is so high.

But let's say we're wearing oxygen tanks and heat-protector suits. We walk along and come to an ocean. Fortunately, our space suits are equipped for deep-sea diving, and we've brought underwater microscopes to help us see super-tiny things. We dive down to the ocean floor and find a world of strange, microscopic creatures. There are beings with tails that whip them along, and others with rows of little bristles moving like oars. There are creatures with shells and harpoons.

Mixed into this zoo are some blue-green creatures—the ancestors of plants. They don't have leaves, seeds, or flowers yet, but like all plants they have learned how to make their own food. They do this by trapping the energy in sunlight. Then they combine that energy with water and carbon dioxide to produce a simple sugar—their food. This process is called photosynthesis. This process also produces oxygen, which is necessary for life. Over many millions of years, these tiny, plantlike forms have slowly released oxygen into the water and air. But the air still

MAGIC GREEN AIR CLEANERS

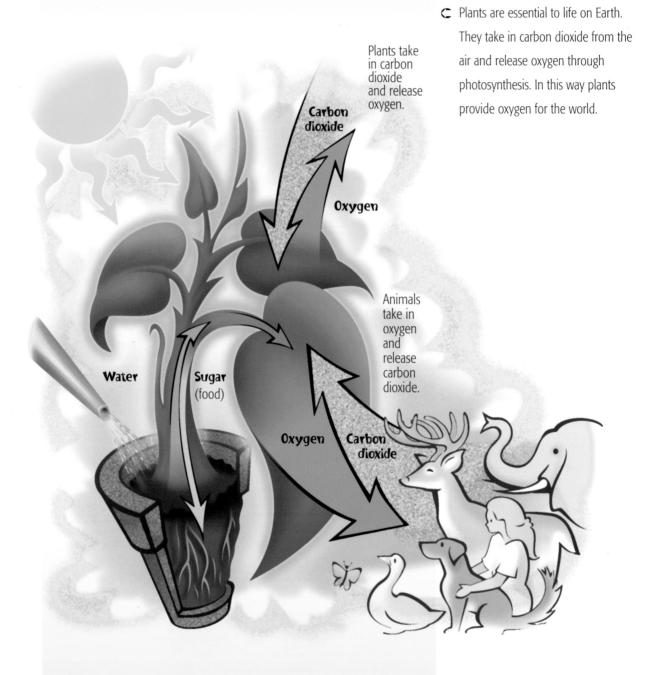

Plants are essential to life on Earth. They take in carbon dioxide from the air and release oxygen through photosynthesis. In this way plants provide oxygen for the world.

Plants take in carbon dioxide and release oxygen.

Carbon dioxide

Oxygen

Animals take in oxygen and release carbon dioxide.

Water

Sugar (food)

Oxygen

Carbon dioxide

contains too little oxygen to support any but the smallest, simplest creatures.

Okay, let's get back in the timeship and travel forward several hundred million years. Now when we step outside, things are more interesting. The Earth's crust has been moving, draining oceans and exposing their plant-rich floors. Plants have been able to spread across the land. There are all kinds of plants, and they're all releasing oxygen into the air. Now we can take off our oxygen masks and just breathe. Because the temperature is cooler now, we can also take off our heat-protector suits.

Looking around, we can see animals, too. Animals have evolved to feed on the plants—first microscopic beings and then larger ones. The animals are breathing in oxygen and breathing out carbon dioxide. The plants are taking in carbon dioxide and releasing oxygen. What a great, harmonious system!

Let's get back in the timeship for our last trip forward to our own time. Now we can see a vast array of different plants and trees. They are still taking in carbon dioxide and supplying the air with oxygen. Billions of years ago they changed the Earth's air by sending oxygen into it. By doing so, they created the essential conditions for life in all its glorious forms.

Earth's Air Blanket

How high do you think the air goes? As high as the moon and stars? No way. Remember Shaq and his basketball? Suppose that basketball were the Earth. If you wound a piece of plastic wrap tightly around the ball, that sheet would be the thickness of the air, where we live and where weather happens.

That layer of air, called the troposphere, reaches only about 11 kilometers (7 miles) above the Earth—that's about the height planes fly at. Beyond that is the rest of the Earth's atmosphere, the mixture of gases that surrounds the planet. The entire atmosphere stretches 2400 kilometers (1500 miles) out into space, but the amount of gases decreases the farther out you go. Plants and animals can only live in the troposphere—the part of the atmosphere we usually mean when we say "air." It has exactly the right mixture of gases, exactly the right temperature, and exactly the right air pressure that living things need. This thin sheet of life-giving air is all we have to keep us breathing. Outside that layer, not even the tiniest microscopic germ can survive. So we shouldn't take this thin sheet of air for granted.

The amount of oxygen in the air begins to decrease even 2 or 3 kilometers (1 or 2 miles) up. Many people find it hard to breathe at those heights. Mountain climbers have to take oxygen with them to climb the highest peaks. And planes flying 10 to 15 kilometers (6 to 9 miles) up have to be specially built to provide normal air for passengers to breathe.

Just as important to Earth creatures as our custom-made blanket of air is another narrow zone just above it. This is the ozone layer. Ozone, a gas formed from oxygen, filters out much of

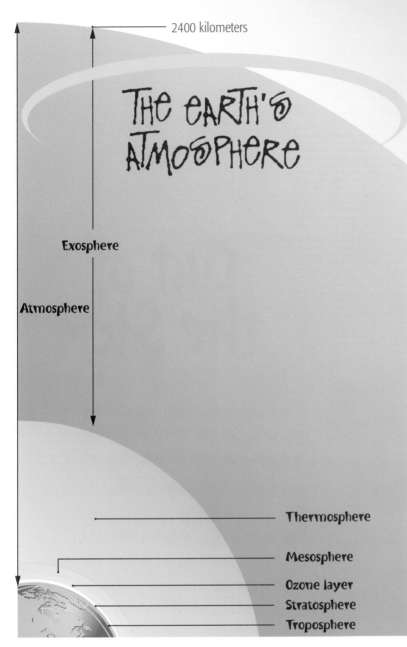

THE EARTH'S ATMOSPHERE

2400 kilometers

Exosphere

Atmosphere

Thermosphere

Mesosphere

Ozone layer

Stratosphere

Troposphere

The atmosphere extends far out into space, but life is possible only in the troposphere. That thin layer of air gives us the perfect temperature, air pressure, and mix of gases we need to live.

the sun's harmful ultraviolet light rays before they strike Earth. Ultraviolet light can damage genes—tiny, invisible elements inside all creatures that make an apple an apple, a butterfly a butterfly, and you you. These invisible "blueprints" also determine what we look like—what color hair and eyes we have, how tall we are, and what shape our nose or mouth is.

Out of the Sky

The Onondaga people tell this legend. According to this story, people first lived in the sky and then came down to Earth.

Long before the Earth was formed, everything was water. Water stretched in every direction, and in it swam all the fish, birds, and animals. Way up above the water was Skyland, which had a beautiful tree with great white roots.

Skyland was ruled by an ancient chief. He had a young wife who was expecting a baby. One night she dreamed that the great tree had been uprooted. When she told her strange dream to the chief, he was very sad.

"That's a powerful dream," he said. "When one has such a powerful dream, it is our way to try to make it come true."

And so the chief wrapped his arms around the trunk of the tree and began to pull. He sweated and strained, and finally the roots gave way. But now where the tree had stood was a huge hole. The chief's wife leaned over the hole and looked out. There, far below, she thought she saw something glistening. She held onto one of the tree's branches for support and leaned over farther. Suddenly she lost her balance and fell through the hole. As she fell down, down, she clutched in her hand some seeds she'd pulled from the tree.

Meanwhile, the animals below looked up.

"Somebody is falling out of Skyland," said a bird.

Right away two swans flew up and brought the chief's wife gently down with their great wings. As they settled onto the water, they let her rest on their backs.

"She is not like us," said one of the swans. "I don't think she can swim or breathe under water. What should we do?"

"I know," said one of the water birds. "I have heard there is Earth far down beneath the water. If someone goes down and pulls up the Earth, then the Sky Lady will have a place to stand."

One after another, the animals and birds and fish dived as far down as they could go. But each time, they came up empty-handed.

Finally, a small voice said, "I will get the Earth or die trying."

It was Muskrat. She was not as big and powerful as some of the animals, but she had a lot of courage. So Muskrat swam down, down, down. She swam so far down that she thought her lungs would burst. But still she swam deeper. Finally, just as her breath ran out, she reached down and touched something. When she floated up to the surface, she held a few bits of Earth in her paw.

"She has the Earth!" the animals shouted in excitement. "Now, where should we put it?"

"Put it on my back," said the Great Turtle.

And so it was done. Immediately the bits of Earth grew bigger and bigger until they became the world. The swans set Sky Lady down on the Earth. As her feet touched the ground, she let the seeds fall out of her hand. Where they fell, trees, grass, and flowers sprang up. And so life began on Earth.

Air Today, Gone Tomorrow?

As you have seen, animals breathe in oxygen and breathe out carbon dioxide. Plants take in carbon dioxide and release oxygen. Together, animals and plants keep our atmosphere in perfect balance. The amazing thing is that this balance has lasted for hundreds of thousands of years.

But now we humans are threatening this balance. About 150 years ago, people started making things in factories. These factories burned fuels such as wood, coal, oil, and gas. It takes air to burn these fuels. When they are burned, they create carbon dioxide, which acts like a pane of glass on a greenhouse—it lets light from the sun through but keeps heat from escaping. That's why greenhouses are so warm.

In the last 100 years, cars and trucks, which also use air and run on oil and gas, have created even more carbon dioxide. We have sent so much carbon dioxide into the air, especially in the last 50 years, that plants can't remove it fast enough and scientists tell us it is raising the Earth's air temperature.

Factories send other harmful gases into the air that endanger the health of people, animals, and plants. If you live in a city, you've probably seen the haze or smelled the fumes of air pollution. This is a big problem all over the world. Not only that, but some of these gases have drifted up to the ozone layer and destroyed parts of it. Space satellites have recorded "holes"—decreases in the amount of ozone—above Antarctica that are twice the size of Europe. This means that more ultraviolet light could be reaching Earth and damaging ocean life, crops, and people.

Fortunately, many countries are trying to stop the damage to our air. Governments are passing laws to control the gases released by factories and cars. New, cleaner fuels are being tested. Many people are riding bikes, taking buses or subways or other forms of public transportation, or using car pools to cut down on the use of cars. All these things can help keep that "air soup" we're in a healthy brew.

We don't know much about how the Earth has kept the air fit for life for so long. But we do know we're changing it. That's mostly because we take air for granted. But when you think about it, you realize that you can't draw a line to mark where the air ends and we begin. The air is part of us. *We are the air.* If we want to keep breathing this life-giving substance, we'll have to remember that. Because whatever we do to the air, we are doing to ourselves.

↺ Riding a bicycle is good for the Earth's health and for yours, too.

Welcome to Planet WaTer

2

If you play lots of sports and have strong muscles, you probably think you're rock solid, right? Well, you're not. You're actually a big blob of water, with just enough solid material to keep you from dribbling away onto the floor!

That's right. You're about 70 percent water. Most is inside your body's cells, the microscopic building blocks that your body is made up of. Cells are largely water. Each cell is enclosed by a thin wall that keeps the water in. The rest of the water in your body flows around outside the cells in various body fluids.

The Earth is mostly water, too. About 74 percent of the planet's surface is covered by water, including oceans, lakes, rivers, and polar ice caps. Even the air is filled with water vapor that condenses, or turns to liquid, forming clouds. We are truly water creatures living on a water planet.

What Water Can Do

So what is this water stuff? You know that some-times it's liquid and sometimes it's solid, when it freezes into ice. And if you boil it in a kettle, it will turn into water vapor, which is a gas. Since you see those things every day, you may think that water is pretty boring. But if you looked at water really closely, through a powerful microscope, you'd find that the water molecule—the smallest part that can still be called water— is downright strange.

Molecules are made of atoms (remember them?) that have electrical charges. Unlike most molecules, the water molecule has negative charges on one side and positive charges on the other side. As a result, it acts as a tiny magnet, attracting other molecules to stick to it. Water molecules stick to each other, and they stick to other kinds of molecules.

Water has many useful features. Because water molecules are attracted to other types of molecules, water can dissolve many minerals (such as salt and rock) and organic materials (such as soil). That's why it is better to wash your clothes in water than in, say, vinegar.

Most useful of all, water can store large amounts of heat and then release it slowly into the air. Because water molecules easily bond to each other, water is very stable. The molecules in other sub-stances are easily disturbed by heating and soon fly off as a gas. But it takes a lot more heat to change water to water vapor. For this rea-son, the oceans can absorb heat in summer and release the heat in winter. The oceans can also absorb heat in the tropics and release the heat in northern areas. So the ability of water to store heat and to move as a liquid is important in affecting weather all over the Earth.

Earth has so much water on it that it's sometimes called the blue planet.

WEIRD WATER

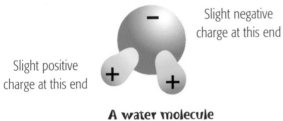

Water molecules have positive and negative charges on opposite sides. For this reason, the molecules easily bond together—the negative sides pull toward the positive sides of other molecules.

Slight negative charge at this end

Slight positive charge at this end

A water molecule

A group of water molecules bonding together

Low temperature

High temperature

A group of water molecules being heated

Low temperature

High temperature

A group of other molecules being heated

WATER ALERT!

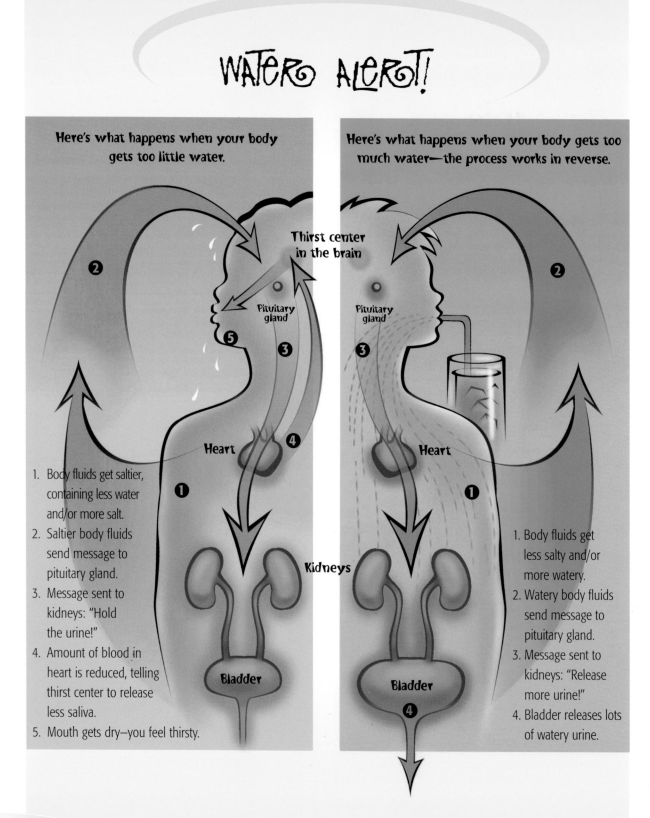

Here's what happens when your body gets too little water.

Thirst center in the brain

Pituitary gland

Heart

Kidneys

Bladder

1. Body fluids get saltier, containing less water and/or more salt.
2. Saltier body fluids send message to pituitary gland.
3. Message sent to kidneys: "Hold the urine!"
4. Amount of blood in heart is reduced, telling thirst center to release less saliva.
5. Mouth gets dry—you feel thirsty.

Here's what happens when your body gets too much water—the process works in reverse.

Pituitary gland

Heart

1. Body fluids get less salty and/or more watery.
2. Watery body fluids send message to pituitary gland.
3. Message sent to kidneys: "Release more urine!"
4. Bladder releases lots of watery urine.

Bladder

Why You Drink All That Milk, Juice, and Pop

You know that cotton ball feeling your mouth gets on a hot summer day, especially when you've been playing hard? That's your body yelling, "Give me water!" If you were lost in a desert without any water, you wouldn't last more than a few days. Next to air, water is your body's most important need.

Your body is a perpetual water recycler. It constantly uses up water in processes such as digestion and releases it in your breath, sweat, tears, urine, or feces. So you have to keep supplying your body with water—about 2.5 liters (quarts) every day for an adult. You get this amount of water from both food and drinks. But the amount of water that goes into your body and the amount that goes out have to be exactly the same, or you're in trouble. Fortunately, unless the situation gets really drastic, the body has an alarm system that keeps the water balance stable.

Water also helps regulate your body's temperature. Did you know that you sweat to cool off? When it is hot, sweat comes out of tiny pores all over your skin. The sweat then evaporates, or changes from a liquid to water vapor. Evaporation takes heat, and that heat is pulled from your body. Try licking your skin and blowing on it to make the moisture evaporate. Feel how cool your skin gets?

Ahaiyuta and the Cloud-Eater

This story is told by the Zuñi people, who have lived for many centuries in the hot deserts of New Mexico.

Long, long ago, on top of a great mountain to the east, lived the monster Cloud-Eater. He'd always had a big appetite for clouds, but for months now he'd been in a cloud-eating frenzy, snatching each one that rolled by with his huge, gaping mouth. Without clouds, there'd been no rain, and the land was dry and baked hard. The cornstalks shriveled in the fields, and the people and their animals were starving.

Far in the west, young Ahaiyuta lived with his grandmother. He was brave and strong, like his father, the Sun. "I must go to the mountain and slay Cloud-Eater," Ahaiyuta said one day. "Then the rains will come, and the people will be happy."

"Be careful!" warned his grandmother. "Cloud-Eater has fought off many fine warriors who tried to kill him. Take these four feathers to help you. But guard them carefully, for they are very powerful. The red feather will lead the way. The blue feather will let you talk with the animals. The yellow feather will make you as small as the tiniest creatures, and the black feather will give you strength for your task."

Ahaiyuta stuck the red feather in his hair, thanked his grandmother, and set off on his long journey. As he walked along, he saw the cracked soil and the brown, dusty cornfields. A blazing sun beat down on him, and he began to feel thirsty, hungry, and very tired. Not a creature stirred.

Suddenly he saw a gopher standing beside its hole. Ahaiyuta stuck the blue and yellow feathers in his hair and in a flash had shrunk down to the size of the gopher.

"Gracious!" said the gopher. "That was an excellent trick! But where are you going in this terrible heat?"

Ahaiyuta told the gopher what he had come to do.

"I will help you," said the gopher. "My home has an underground passage leading right to Cloud-Eater's mountain. I will take you to him."

Ahaiyuta followed the gopher into its hole. They ran swiftly along the tunnel, which took a steep climb as they reached the mountain. At last they could hear the monster snoring just above them. "Wait here," said the gopher. He scampered ahead, tunneling through the dirt until he broke through to where the monster was lying. He began to gnaw the fur that covered the monster's heart.

"Whazzat?" asked the monster sleepily.

"Don't worry, Grandfather," the gopher replied.

"I'm just taking a few hairs to line my nest. You'll never miss them."

The gopher ran back to Ahaiyuta and told him what he'd done. "The tunnel leads right to Cloud-Eater's heart," he said. "Aim well—and good luck!"

Ahaiyuta put the black feather in his hair and crept along the tunnel until he saw his target. He placed an arrow in his bow, aimed carefully, and then—strike! Immediately great roars and shrieks filled the air. The earth shook and rocks tumbled as Cloud-Eater thrashed about in his bed. Finally all was still.

"Cloud-Eater has eaten his last cloud!" cried Ahaiyuta. "Now the rains will surely come."

The gopher and Ahaiyuta ran back through the tunnel to the entrance. When they emerged, dark clouds already covered the Sun, and large drops of rain were beginning to fall. Soon rain was pouring from the sky, soaking the Earth with its nourishing gifts. Ahaiyuta thanked the gopher and waved good-bye. As streams of water swirled about his feet, he laughed with delight and began to run. He knew that he had saved his people and that he would be known as a great hero.

How Water Gets Around

After your sweat goes into the air, what do you suppose happens to it? Well, in a few months the moisture might turn up in a drenching rain storm or a snowstorm or land in the ocean. Or if a molecule of your sweat fell on the ground, it might get slurped up by a tree rootlet, travel all the way to a leaf, and be released into the air from there. That's because you don't just recycle your body's water. You're part of a much larger, grander show—the Earth's great water cycle.

Like you, all the other animals on Earth need water. And if you've ever watched a plant grow, you know that plants need water, too. The tropical rain forests are an especially important part of the water cycle. They are like giant sponges that draw in huge amounts of water. They hold it in the soil with their giant root systems, they use it to grow and make food, and they send it back up into the clouds through their leaves.

Rain or snow falls onto land.

⊃ Water is always on the move. Water from your sweat and from oceans and rivers evaporates into the atmosphere. Some of that water forms clouds. Then rain or snow falls, soaking into the ground and filling up rivers and oceans. Some water in the ground is drawn up by plant rootlets, where it makes its way to leaves, and from there goes back into the atmosphere.

EARTH'S WATER DANCE

Clouds condense.

Energy from the sun
causes water to
evaporate.

Water returns
to the atmosphere.

Water seeps into
the ground.

Ocean

Water runs into streams.

How Water Learned to Dance

Water has not always existed on Earth. It developed gradually over hundreds of millions of years. In the very beginning, Earth was a fiery planet—so hot that water couldn't have existed in a liquid form. It would have all turned to water vapor after being blown up into the air from volcanoes.

A few million years later, though, when the world had cooled down a bit, water vapor began to form clouds. Eventually this water vapor fell as rain. After a few more million years, rain was pouring down onto a landscape of rocky mountains and deep valleys. After many more millions of years, fresh water covered most of the Earth. It began to dissolve and wash away mineral salts in the rock. Finally, large seas of salty water were created.

Then, more then three billion years ago, the first life-forms—very simple, bacteria-like organisms—appeared in the oceans. And now that life was here, the great water dance could begin.

A Very Fresh Story

If you've ever swallowed a mouthful of ocean water by mistake, you know how salty it is. And that's where more than 97 percent of the Earth's water is—in the oceans. What humans and most other animals and plants need to survive is unsalty water, or fresh water. We need it for drinking, washing, and irrigating our food crops. One of the marvels of the water cycle is that it changes salty water from the oceans into the fresh water we need. When the sun's rays heat the oceans, water vapor rises into the sky, leaving the salt behind. Then water vapor falls back to Earth as rain or snow, refilling the streams and soaking deep into the ground.

Rain constantly renews the Earth's supply of fresh water. But that doesn't mean the supply is endess. Most of the Earth's fresh water is frozen in glaciers or buried deep underground. Compared with all the water on Earth, the amount of drinking water we have access to—in rivers, lakes, and wells—is very small.

Supplies of fresh water vary enormously in different parts of the world. Canada is lucky to have a lot in its many rivers and lakes, although not all of it is accessible. But in many other countries, fresh water is scarce. The central part of Australia, for example, is mostly a desert. As a result, almost all the people in Australia live along the south coast.

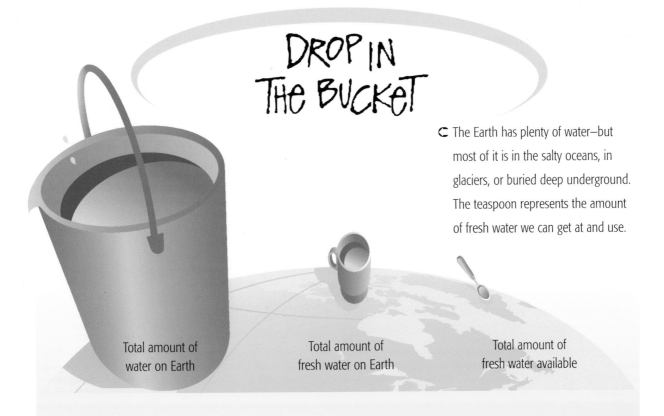

DROP IN THE BUCKET

℃ The Earth has plenty of water—but most of it is in the salty oceans, in glaciers, or buried deep underground. The teaspoon represents the amount of fresh water we can get at and use.

Total amount of water on Earth

Total amount of fresh water on Earth

Total amount of fresh water available

A FOGGY DRINK

Have you ever taken a drink of fog? Trees and plants do it all the time. Fog is a ground-level cloud of tiny water droplets, so small and light that they float in the air and get blown by the wind. When a few million of these droplets hit something, such as a tree leaf, they condense and run down it as water. Before long, the tree and the soil beneath it have soaked up a lot of fog water.

Taking a tip from the trees, Canadian scientist Robert Schemenauer worked with Chilean scientists to invent a device that collects fog water in much the same way. Two poles are sunk into the ground with a mesh screen stretched upright between them. The mesh is 50 percent fiber and 50 percent holes to let just the right amount of wind get through. Since wind blows fog in a sideways direction, the water droplets hit the upright screen and run down. The water collects in a trough at the bottom of the screen. Pipes lead from the trough to a storage tank.

Fog collection is a simple, relatively inexpensive way to bring water to high, dry areas where water is scarce or polluted. The biggest system so far is at El Tofo, on a high coastal ridge in Chile.

There 88 collectors supply 13,000 liters (quarts) of water a day to the remote fishing village of Chungungo. The people used to pay a lot for water brought in by truck from 40 kilometers (25 miles) away. Many families could only buy a few liters a day. Now they have taps in their homes that provide clean water for drinking, washing, and cooking, and the town is blooming with gardens and fruit trees.

Animals have also found ways to survive in the driest areas. Desert camels, for example, store fat in their humps. The fat then breaks down to create water. Camels also manage to excrete as little water as possible—their urine is almost like crystal (ouch!). The African lungfish sleeps through the hot summer. And the African fog-basking beetle has learned the fog-drinking trick. On foggy days it crouches down with its back up in the air and lets the fog droplets run down into its mouth.

Eighty-eight fog collectors at El Tofo, Chile, bring fresh, unpolluted water to the people of Chungungo.

Water Down the Drain

No creature is as clever as humans in finding ways to capture, move, store, and especially use water. In the rich countries of North America, people use vast amounts of water in their homes for drinking, cooking, cleaning, and watering their lawns. And factories use a lot of water to make all the things we buy. They use water, for instance, to generate electricity, to mix chemicals, to wash away waste materials, and to move wood fibers in pulp.

Think about dinnertime at your place. Perhaps you drink a glass of water with your meal. There's also the water used to grow your vegetables and the water power that may be used to generate the electricity that turns on your lights. Then there's the water used by the factories that made your dishes, knives and forks, tablecloth, and table. And don't forget washing the dishes—and the factories that made the dish detergent and its plastic bottle.

⊂ People control and use the Earth's water resources in many ways. Hydroelectric dams harness the power of water to generate electricity.

HOW LAURA AND LOSERO USE WATER

Laura

Laura lives in Buffalo, New York. Here's how she might use water on a typical day.

- Brush teeth.
- Flush toilet (several times).
- Wash hands and face in sink.
- At school, clean up after art class.
- Drink from water fountain (three times).
- Wash hands before lunch.
- Fill hamster's water bottle in science class.
- Drink bottle of water after gym class.
- Go swimming after school.
- Shower after swim.
- Wash hands before dinner.
- Refill dog's water dish.
- Brush teeth.
- Take hot bath.

Losero

Losero lives in a village in Kenya. Here's how he might use water in a day.

- Drink mug of tea for breakfast.
- Take drink of water from well at school.
- After school, fill water trough for family's cattle.
- Wash hands before main meal of the day.
- Drink glass of water after meal.

Water use varies greatly from country to country. Americans and Canadians each use an average of up to 1000 liters (quarts) of water every day. In Kenya, many people get by on only 5 liters a day.

Besides using so much of our precious water, we also pollute it. We use our oceans, lakes, and rivers as sewers, dumping human, farm, and factory waste into them. We build huge dams and canals so that ships can sail in from all over the world. We cut down forests lining the shores of rivers and lakes and build cities there. All these activities can pollute water and harm the health of people, other animals, plants, and entire ecosystems.

An ecosystem is a community of plants, animals, soil, and water—all interacting and depending on each other to survive in a certain place, such as a lake or prairie. If too much waste is poured into a lake, the water can become unsafe for people to drink. It can kill fish or give them diseases that make them unfit to eat. Human activities such as building dams and cutting down forests can destroy whole ecosystems that plants and animals had depended on for water, nesting places, and food.

People in North America, especially, use water as if it will never run out. But the first North Americans—the Native people who had lived here for thousands of years when the Europeans arrived—thought of water as sacred. The great waterways provided food, water, and transportation. They were precious gifts to be respected and treated with care. These peoples believed that the oceans, rivers, and streams were part of them, and that they needed them to survive.

And you know something? They were right. Not only do we need water, *we are water*. Water fills our bodies, is used in body processes such as digestion, and constantly passes through us as part of the Earth's great water cycle. Water is a precious gift we must care for if we care for ourselves.

Getting Down to Earth

3

Three-quarters of the planet may be covered by water, but you and I live on good old, solid earth, right? Earth, soil, ground, land—whatever you call it, it's as common as—well, dirt.

When you were a little kid, didn't you love digging in the dirt, making mud pies? You might even have tried a taste. But now you'd probably rather grab a slice of pizza or scarf down a hunk of chocolate cake with thick, gooey frosting. Did you know that both that cake and the pizza came from dirt? In fact, just about everything you eat comes from the soil.

DINING ON DIRT

Say you had a ham sandwich, an apple, and milk for lunch one day. Here's how the whole thing came from the soil.

Fuel Up

As you can see, every bit of this lunch not only came from dirt but was once a living plant or animal. (Okay, all except the salt, which is a chemical.) The same is true of all the food you eat. You are basically a compost heap for dead things! After you put that food in your mouth, your body does a wonderful job of grinding and mixing and mushing it all up into a gloppy soup. And that gets broken down further into nutrients the body needs for life itself.

The most important of these nutrients are fats, proteins, and carbohydrates. To be healthy, you need to get enough of them every day, together with water, fiber, and certain vitamins and minerals. Most foods you eat contain several of these nutrients. A peanut butter sandwich on whole wheat bread, for example, contains most of them. So it's easier to choose a healthy diet if you think of foods rather than nutrients.

THE FABULOUS FOUR

⊂ Scientists have divided foods into four groups according to the nutrients they contain.

4 **Meat & alternatives**
(2-3 servings)

3 **Milk products**
(3-4 servings)

2 **Vegetables & fruits**
(5-6 servings)

1 **Grain products**
(5-8 servings)

GULP!

How a bowl of chili gives you great hair

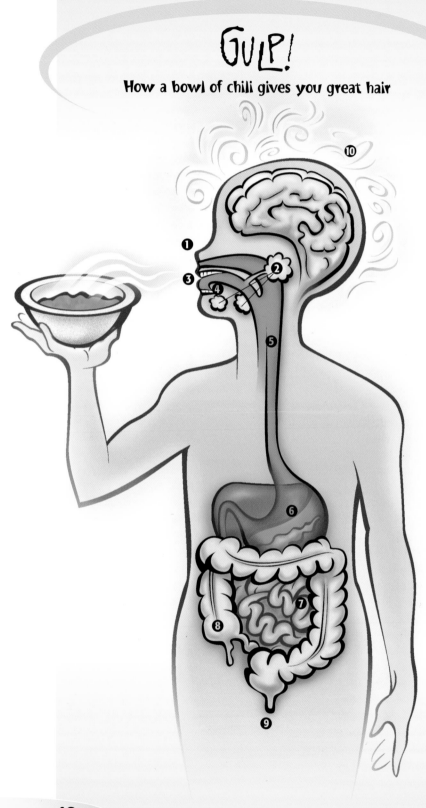

1. Nose smells chili.

2. Salivary glands release saliva. Saliva moistens food.

3. Teeth chew food into softened lumps.

4. Tongue sends lumps of food down throat.

5. Food moves from esophagus to stomach.

6. Digestive juices break down fats and proteins.

7. Liquid food passes into small intestine, which breaks down carbohydrates and absorbs nutrients and water.

8. Food not absorbed into body passes into large intestine.

9. Large intestine releases remaining food products from body.

10. Absorbed nutrients pass into your blood and are carried to all parts of your body, including your hair.

How Soil Got That Way

How far down does the ground go? Do you think it goes right to the center of the Earth? Actually, it's a very thin layer. If the Earth were a giant tomato, 70 meters (77 yards) around in the middle, the soil would be far thinner than the skin of a regular tomato. Below that thin layer is solid rock and hot liquid rock.

That skinny covering coat of soil wasn't always there. Like air and water, soil evolved gradually over billions of years. Let's get back into our timeship and find out how that happened.

Okay, we're back in the early days of the Earth, when hot melted rock was beginning to cool and harden into solid rock. It's a good thing we have our heat-proof suits on, because it's still fiery hot. But there's no soil anywhere, so let's not hang around here. In a few million years, things are going to get a lot more interesting—not to mention more comfortable.

Now it's hundreds of millions of years later, and we can see how wind, rain, and snow have begun to break down the rock. The smaller chunks are being moved across the surface of the Earth by wind, glaciers, gravity, and running water. And as they move, the chunks are getting smaller. This process is called weathering. And amazingly, over many millions of years, weathering can wear down mountains and turn boulders into sand.

Back in our timeship now, we'll zoom ahead to about 3.5 billion years ago and have a look at one of the oceans. Our ship, of course, is totally seaworthy and can sail to the bottom like a submarine. Look—the ocean floor is covered in fine silt. This silt was created when water up on land weathered certain types of rock into powdery bits and washed them out to sea. And the first tiny

life-forms have been born in the ocean brew. Some are making it up onto land. Masses of those microorganisms are invading cracks in the rock, looking for nutrients. That pressure is breaking down the rock, too. On land there is now sand, clay, dust, and gravel, but still no soil.

We take another big jump ahead in our timeship, to 350 million years ago. Now plants have moved out of the oceans. Together with bacteria, they're really going to town on the rocks. To anchor themselves, plants have crumbled rock by sending their roots deep into any holes they could find. Bacteria have released chemicals that have dissolved rock and produced nutrients they could use. And what's this over here? Zillions of bacteria and plants have died over the years, and their bodies have added to the powdered rock. A little mound of brown crumbly stuff has formed. The breakdown of life-forms has finally created soil.

Let's zoom ahead a few more million years. As dead matter and broken-down rocks and minerals have piled up, the soil has in many places become richer and deeper. Over time, larger plants like trees and bigger animals added their bodies after their deaths to the soil. Thus, their bodies enriched the soil just as the soil nourished them.

Time to go home now to the present. Let's take a quick trip around our planet. (Conveniently, our timeship is also a spaceship.) As we speed around the globe, we see a fabulous variety of plants, trees, mammals, insects, and other creatures forming a multitude of different communities—prairie grasslands, Arctic wetlands, tropical rain forests. And the soils that nourish them are different, too. Soils and creatures have helped create each other.

The Myth of Gaia

The early Greeks told this story to show how important soil is.

Gaia was the great mother-goddess of the Earth, the provider and creator of all things. She created Uranus, god of the heavens, and together they peopled the universe. She made the storm-spirits and other forces of nature, as well as human beings.

One of Gaia's granddaughters was Demeter, who later took on some of the Earth Mother's role as the goddess of planted soil, fertility, and the harvest. Demeter had a daughter, Persephone. One day, as Persephone was gathering flowers in a sunlit field, she was kidnapped by her uncle Hades, king of the underworld. Hades' kingdom was the fearful home of the dead, but it was also the source of life and growth. When Persephone disappeared underground, all growth stopped on Earth.

Demeter searched all over the world for her lost daughter. Finally Hades agreed to return her to her mother so that harvests could begin again. But unknown to Persephone, the gods had proclaimed that if she ate any food in the underworld, she would have to remain there forever. To keep her with him, cunning Hades offered her a seed of the pomegranate as a parting gift. Persephone ate it, and so was ordered to return to Hades' realm for part of every year. But in the spring she would return again, bringing new life to the Earth.

Ever since that time, leaves and plants have returned to the dark soil to bloom again in spring. Each year the world must die to be reborn again from the Earth, the mother of us all.

The Soil
Is Alive

If you have a garden, you could try this. Fill an empty 1-liter (1-quart) milk carton with garden soil. Dump it out onto a piece of newspaper and have a good look. Use a magnifying glass if you have one. See any living creatures? You'll probably find dozens of small crawly things—earthworms, beetles, and ants. But that's not even the half of it.

If you had a microscope, you'd see that the soil is crammed with tiny organisms and that the whole pile is moving! You'd see countless different kinds of bacteria alone, plus untold numbers of algae, fungi, nematodes, mites, and springtails. A mere pinch of soil—what you could hold between two fingers—could contain as many as a million fungi and over a billion bacteria.

Soil is full of living things. All these microscopic plants and animals are feeding on other soil creatures, mixing air and moisture into the soil, and enriching it with their dead bodies. They are busy fertilizing the soil—making it rich and healthy for new plants to grown in. There are so many billions of these microorganisms in the soil that in some areas, they are the major lifeforms. Geologists have drilled down 4 kilometers (2.5 miles) below the surface of the Earth and even found microorganisms in solid rock. Scientists estimate that the total weight of all microorganisms on Earth is greater than the weight of all other plants and animals combined.

Just as amazing as the tiny soil creatures are the giant ones. You won't find any giant animals underground, but you will find plants and fungi. Trees are the largest plants on Earth, and some are truly colossal. The tallest trees of the rain forests soar more than 50 meters (160 feet) into the air, and the giant redwoods of California have trunks wide enough to drive a car through. But what's underground is sometimes even more amazing. Tree roots dig deep into the soil, branching out into smaller and smaller rootlets in their search for moisture. The total length of the root system of a single tree can measure hundreds of kilometers!

Some fungi spread out like nets, covering hectares of land. Fungi are a group of organisms similar to plants, but they don't photosynthesize and they reproduce by spores rather than by seeds. Some common fungi are mushrooms, mold, and yeast.

This mass of life, both big and small, depends on the soil, just as soil depends on it. It is one more example of nature's pattern of connections.

With trees, what you don't see is as big as or bigger than what you do see. Tree roots tunnel deep into the soil, searching out precious moisture and nutrients. ↻

Sacred Soil

Soil directly supplies 98 percent of the world's food. Even though fish is a staple in the diet of many cultures, most people in the world live primarily on grains, such as rice, corn, and wheat. Humans have depended on plants and soil for food ever since we first appeared on Earth.

The early peoples thought of the Earth—both planet and soil—as sacred. Earth was home and the provider of life. Since the Earth cared for them, they respected and cared for the Earth. Native people still have this idea today. They often refer to "Mother Earth" because it gives birth to all life.

But most of the world has a different view. Rather than honoring the Earth, we often destroy it. The Earth's precious topsoil—the thin, fertile upper layer—was formed over thousands of years as generations of plants and animals died and enriched it with their bodies. But now the world's supply of topsoil is shrinking. Although nature creates new fertile soil every year, we destroy 23 billion tonnes more than is made. We do this by cutting down forests and allowing the soil underneath to be swept away by wind and rain. We do it by paving over more and more of our best farmland to put up buildings and parking lots. Mostly we do it by using harmful farming methods.

Most of the food you eat comes from huge farms where the aim is to produce more and bigger crops as fast as possible. To achieve this, farmers douse their fields with powerful fertilizers and pesticides. The chemicals in these products pollute the air, the ground, and any nearby water. They also kill many of the soil microorganisms that create new soil. Farmers on these

Dakota children understand that we are of the soil and the soil of us, that we have the birds and beasts that grew with us on this soil. A bond exists between all things because they all drink the same water and breathe the same air.

–Luther Standing Bear,
My People the Sioux

factory-like farms often plant the same crop over and over, not allowing enough time between plantings for soil to become fertile again naturally. At the same time, the world's population is growing by 90 million people a year, meaning that even more fertile land is needed to grow food. To meet that need, forests are being rapidly cut down and the soil used for planting crops. Cutting down trees for farmland is a major cause of forest loss throughout the world.

But many people are concerned about the soil. Organic farmers try to use nature's own methods to grow food and keep soil healthy. For example, they fertilize the soil with compost (dead plants) and plant a variety of crops. They don't use chemical pesticides. Instead, they use bacteria that kill insects without harming other animals. Figuring out how nature does things is not easy, since every area has its own ecosystem, in which soil and weather and plants and animals are connected to each other in a very complex way. But it's a start.

Have you heard the expression "You are what you eat"? It's meant as a kind of joke, but it's scientifically true. And since everything you eat comes from the soil, it's also true that just as you are air and water, *you are also the Earth.* That's a good reason to honor it and treat it well.

Fire Power

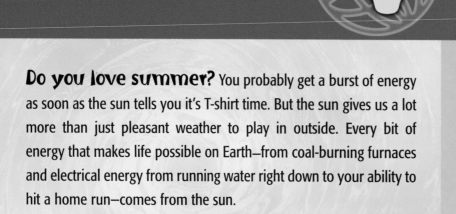

4

Do you love summer? You probably get a burst of energy as soon as the sun tells you it's T-shirt time. But the sun gives us a lot more than just pleasant weather to play in outside. Every bit of energy that makes life possible on Earth—from coal-burning furnaces and electrical energy from running water right down to your ability to hit a home run—comes from the sun.

Plugging into the Sun

What is energy? Scientists describe it as the ability to do work. And work means any kind of activity. Scientists have learned that energy can't be created out of nothing; it has to be obtained from somewhere else.

For example, suppose you want to hammer a nail into a piece of wood. The energy you need to do that comes from energy stored in your body. That energy comes from the food you've eaten. (Remember the chili drawing?) And the energy in the food came from the sun. If you've ever planted vegetables in the garden or a pot of flowers on the windowsill, you know that plants need sunlight to grow.

But back to the nail. When you hit the nail, the energy is transferred to it in the form of motion (the nail goes into the wood) and heat. You can feel the warmth in the nail for a second or two. Then the heat spreads out into the wood and air. Although it isn't lost, it is no longer available to do work—it has decayed. Energy in the world is always decaying like that. Fortunately, the sun constantly floods the Earth with energy to recharge its batteries.

All living things need the sun's energy. Plants and animals need energy to grow and reproduce. You need energy to move, to see, to breathe. You need a little energy just to lie in the grass, thinking deep thoughts. Even when you're sleeping, your body is giving off as much heat as a 100-watt lightbulb.

When you hammer a nail into a block of wood, you're using "mechanical" energy (muscle power). After you hit the nail, that energy changes to heat energy, which goes into the nail, wood, and air.

Mechanical energy (the energy of motion)

Heat energy

56

Your Top-of-the-Line Inner Furnace

Have you ever shivered with cold on a frosty morning or sweltered in the heat of a summer afternoon? As miserable as the outer you—toes, fingers, skin—might have felt, the deepest part of your body was a comfortable 37°C (98°F) the whole time. That's because your body-core temperature stays about the same, whatever the outside temperature may be. This constant inner temperature keeps your body's engines—blood circulation, breathing, digestion, and so on—humming along smoothly.

Your body has three main ways of keeping the inner you nice and toasty.

The first is metabolism, the body's main source of heat. Metabolism is the process that breaks down nutrients such as fats, carbohydrates, and proteins into simpler materials, releasing energy for the body's work. Besides keeping you warm, this energy is used for growth and the repair of body cells and tissues.

Your body's second source of heat is your skin, which absorbs heat. You lose heat through your skin, too. If the air is cold, you can lose up to one-third of your body heat through exposed skin.

Your third source of body heat is muscle activity. As you know, playing hockey on a cold day warms you up, while too much running around on a hot day makes you feel even hotter. Up to 90 percent of your body heat can come from moving your muscles.

When it's really freezing outside, you might stomp your feet and wave your arms around. And something else happens—you shiver. That's a kind of muscular activity, too. Receptors in your skin sense the cold air and send signals to the "shivering center"

TAKING THE HEAT

Your skin is a natural "heat-protector suit," helping to keep the inner you at just the right temperature. Skin absorbs heat through the flow of air or water over it, from radiating sources such as the sun or fire, and through contact with hot things.

Flow of hot water over skin

A radiating source

Direct contact with a hot surface

in your brain. It tells your muscles to move, creating heat. Your brain also relays the message to tiny muscles inside your blood vessels, telling them to shrink. That cuts down the blood flow to your skin, hands, and feet and keeps it where it counts most—in your inner core. You have tiny muscles at the base of your hair roots that also contract, and then brrrr—goose bumps.

If you're too hot, blood vessels near your skin expand. That increases the blood flow from your center to your skin, and the blood brings heat with it. Your skin becomes flushed, and then you sweat. Water is released through special sweat glands—you have about 2.5 million of them all over your skin. The sweat evaporates into the air, taking body heat with it.

These methods work well as long as temperature changes aren't too great. In extreme cold, the body tries to keep the core temperature at 37°C (98°F) by shivering and breathing harder. But if it drops to about 30°C (86°F), we stop moving and lose consciousness. At about 24°C (76°F), we die. Similarly, if our core temperature rises even a few degrees above normal, we're in danger. The heat of a fever is one way the body fights infection, because heat kills many kinds of germs. But it can kill us, too.

Old Flames Still Keep Us Warm

Scientists think our earliest human-like ancestors learned how to start a fire over a million years ago. They lived in tropical Africa then, where the climate was warm enough to get by without a fire. But once they had fire, humans were able to spread out to colder climates all over the world.

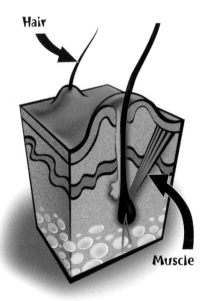

⌒ When you are cold, muscles near the roots of your hair contract, giving you goose bumps.

Learning to start a fire was a great technical achievement—one of the first of many to come. And like all technology, it's had both good and bad sides. A bonfire can keep us warm and cook our hot dogs. But it can also rage out of control and burn us up.

For many thousands of years, people burned animal fat, animal droppings, straw, and wood in their fires. Then, just a few hundred years ago, they started using coal, which they dug out from the ground. Oil and natural gas were discovered only about 200 years ago. In that short time the whole world has become dependent on coal, oil, and natural gas for heating, cooking, and running machines, especially cars and trucks. And we are rapidly using up the Earth's supply of these three fuels. Scientists have estimated, for example, that at the present rate of use, all Earth's sources of oil will be gone in just 35 years. And it took about 400 million years to form!

Coal, gas, and oil are called fossil fuels. That's because like fossils, these fuels were formed from the remains of prehistoric plants and animals. Very slowly, over hundreds of millions of years, the bodies of dead plants and animals piled up layer upon layer. They were gradually changed by pressure and by chemical processes. Because the bodies were once living things, they had heat energy from the sun stored in them. And that heat can be recovered when oil, coal, and gas are used as fuel.

In other words, your family's car runs on the remains of creatures that lived long before the dinosaur age. Coal, oil, and gas are one-time gifts. When these fuels are gone, there won't be any more—at least not for another few hundred million years.

The Gift of Prometheus

This myth from the early Greeks shows the double-sided nature of fire.

Since the beginning of time, Zeus, the supreme god, had kept fire for the gods' use alone. But one day Prometheus, who was a cunning rogue, stole it and brought it down to men on Earth. (There were no women then.) Zeus was enraged by this bold crime and condemned Prometheus to a gruesome punishment. He was chained to a mountainside for eternity, and every day an eagle came and tore out his liver.

The men were not spared Zeus's fury either. Zeus couldn't take fire away from them, so he gave them something else just as tricky. He created Pandora, the first woman (whose name meant "all gifts") and sent her down to Earth carrying a sealed box, which she was forbidden to open.

Like fire, Pandora was enchantingly beautiful, but she was also uncontrollably curious. One day Pandora opened the box, and out swarmed Zeus's "gifts"—a horde of miseries such as disease, rage, despair, and old age. These miseries would plague humans forever after.

This myth may remind you of the Garden of Eden story. Both tales suggest that as human beings reach out for knowledge and power, they sometimes get more than they bargained for.

Playing with Fire

In nature, plants and animals use and pass on energy to each other in a continuous cycle. For example, the dung beetle lays its eggs in animal droppings, or dung. When the eggs hatch, the dung provides nutrients for the baby beetles. The beetles may then become food for a toad, who may be eaten by a snake. The snake may be eaten by a fox, which will leave dung, dung beetles will lay their eggs in it, and so the circle begins again. Because one animal's waste is used by another animal, nothing is wasted. The energy keeps getting used and passed on.

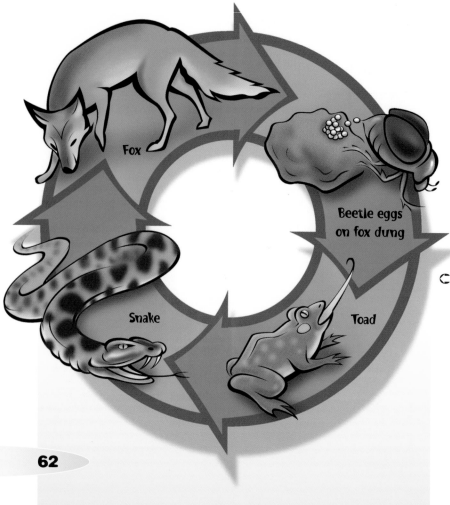

Fox

Beetle eggs on fox dung

Snake

Toad

Nature uses energy in a circular pattern, with no waste left over. But people often use energy in a straight line, creating plenty of waste products that pollute the air, water, and soil. You could say we've got a problem with our waste line! ⊃

Only humans use energy in a way that produces waste. We use energy in a straight line rather than a circle. Using fossil fuels to heat our homes and run our factories and cars creates dangerous waste products that cannot be used but must be disposed of.

Nitrogen and sulfur gases pollute the air we breathe and fall to Earth to damage soil, water, and trees. Fossil fuels also release carbon dioxide, which traps heat. Plants use carbon dioxide in photosynthesis. But because we are burning so much fossil fuel today, more carbon dioxide is being released than all the plants in the world can use, and it's building up. Scientists believe this buildup is causing changes in climate that could have disastrous effects.

It is also foolish to depend on fuels that can't be replaced. Trees will grow again, but coal, oil, and gas won't.

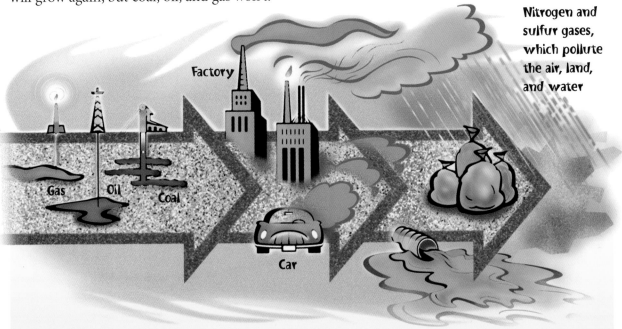

Nitrogen and sulfur gases, which pollute the air, land, and water

Gas

Oil

Coal

Factory

Car

HOW MATT AND MUNA USE ENERGY

Matt

Matt lives in Canada. A day in Matt's life might go something like this.

- Matt gets up and switches on bedside radio.
- Goes into bathroom and turns on lights.
- In kitchen, makes piece of toast in toaster as Mom or Dad cooks his cereal on stove.
- Gets on school bus.
- In school, uses computer in fluorescent-lit classroom.
- After school, gets can of pop from fridge.
- Does homework while watching TV.
- Eats dinner with family, beneath light hanging over table.
- Plays video game.
- Goes to bed and reads comics with flashlight under covers.

Muna

Muna lives in a small village in Nepal. Her day would go more like this.

- Muna gets up and helps her mother make fire in depression in floor of hut (mud floor, thatched roof).
- Carries hay out to oxen in shed.
- Walks to school.
- Writes in notebook by light coming in window; there are no electric lights.
- After school, helps with the work of her family's farm by gathering firewood. She carries a big bundle of it on her back.
- At home, eats with family by candlelight.
- Goes to bed.

On average, each person in developed countries such as Canada uses as much energy in six months as a citizen of developing countries such as Nepal uses in his or her entire lifetime.

Save Your Energy

What can we do? For a start, we can stop wasting energy. We can do this in simple ways, such as turning off lights when we aren't using them, lowering the thermostats in our homes at night, and using energy-efficient fluorescent lights whenever possible. We can also walk, skate, or bike more instead of riding in cars. It's a lot more fun to do these things, and it's good for our health and the Earth's health, too.

We can also make bigger changes as communities and nations. Instead of relying on fossil fuels, we can use energy sources that don't pollute and will never run out. For instance, in places near the ocean, the power of tides can drive turbines, which are wheel-like devices with blades that help them rotate. The turbines are connected to generators, which produce electricity. In windy regions, wind can also drive turbines to produce electricity. And best of all, the bountiful power of sunlight can be captured to heat and light homes, heat water, and generate electricity. Perhaps you have a calculator or a game that uses solar power. These sources of energy are being used in small ways today but show promise of having much wider uses in the future.

Like all living things, we share in the Earth's stores of energy. That energy comes from the sun—Earth's fiery star—and burns in every cell of our bodies. Because we need the sun's gifts to live, we must learn to use them wisely because *we are sunlight*.

ℂ Solar panels use the sun's energy to generate electricity for lighting, heating, or hot water.

Depending on Our Relatives

5

Did you know that you have about six billion creatures living on your body? They especially like to hang out on your forehead, where there is a good supply of oil to shield them from the air. Some prefer to nestle in your eyelashes.

No, we're not talking about lice, ticks, or fleas. We're talking about bacteria and other tiny organisms you'd need a microscope to see. Everybody has them, and you can't get rid of them. Even if you stood in the shower all day, more would land on you from the air seconds after you came out. They like you because you're a great host. You provide them with all kinds of tasty morsels to feed on—skin flakes, oil, dirt, and each other. But don't worry—most of them are harmless. They're just feeding, breeding, living, and growing in their habitat. Plants and animals do the same thing in forest, tidepool, prairie, or desert habitats. And we need these bugs.

Your body is a miniature ecosystem. To these bugs, you're part of their environment, just as the town you live in is part of your environment.

But Do We Really Need 750,000 Kinds of Insects?

The creatures on your body aren't all the same. They include dozens of different species, or kinds, of organism. Scientists estimate that the Earth is home to 10 to 15 million species of plants and animals. One of them is the species you belong to—the human species, or *Homo sapiens*. In the history of life on Earth, about 30 billion species are thought to have existed. Today, 99.9 percent of these species are extinct—gone forever, like the dinosaurs.

Earth's present family, though, is truly amazing. Great horned owls, African elephants, domestic cats, chestnut trees, killer whales, ladybugs, McIntosh apples—our relatives come in an incredible number of forms. There's a word for that tremendous variety—*biodiversity*. *Bio* means life, and *diversity* means difference. The idea of biodiversity includes not only beings as different as pigs and pine trees but also many different kinds of pigs and pines. Scientists have discovered about 290,000 species of beetles alone, and they think that's only a small proportion of the total number that exists. This abundance of species is not an accident or a waste. Like air, water, soil, and energy from the sun, it seems that biodiversity is necessary for life.

All of nature is interconnected. Like the water cycle and the yearly return of the seasons, the lives of all animals and plants are connected in a circular pattern. As one creature is born, it feeds and depends on other creatures, and when it dies, it nourishes and maintains still others.

The Pacific Salmon's Great Circle Game

Salmon alevins are hatched. Later, the young fish, now known as fry, eat small freshwater creatures such as insects, snails, and worms.

Eggs are fertilized.

Roots of trees in the forest hold the soil of the riverbanks and keep it from wearing away.

Fry also provide food for birds and larger fish.

Leaves fall into the stream and feed bacteria, which are eaten by insects, which in turn are eaten by fish.

The bigger the salmon run, the bigger the animal population, and the more fertile the soil will be for forest growth.

When they are one month to three years old, salmon travel to the ocean.

In the ocean, salmon feed on small ocean creatures.

Salmon are food for killer whales, eagles, and seals.

After two to six years in the ocean, salmon swim back to the stream where they were born and spawn, which means to lay eggs.

After spawning, the salmon die. Their bodies nourish bacteria, fungi, and other organisms that the fry feed on. So the fry are living off molecules that came from their parents!

So the river, the ocean, the forest, the soil, the salmon, and all the other creatures benefit each other. This is just one example of nature's circular pattern. All 10 to 15 million species on Earth today are connected through their life cycles. Everything depends on everything else. Like nuts and bolts in an aircraft, each species is necessary for the health of spaceship Earth.

More Is Better for Ecosystems

Having many species is a great advantage to whole ecosystems when conditions change—say, when the climate becomes drier or a new species arrives. For example, tropical rain forests are crammed with living things. Just a few hectares contain as many species of trees as there are in all of North America. If an insect pest invades a Brazilian rain forest, it meets an army of birds, reptiles, and small mammals that compete with it for space, feed on it, and keep it from spreading beyond a small area. But a temperate rain forest in Washington or in British Columbia has far fewer species. When an insect pest such as the spruce budworm invades one of these forests, there aren't so many species to try to stop it. The insect pest can get a foothold and then destroy huge areas of forest.

Scattered over the Earth is a patchwork of ecosystems—coral reefs, tundra, wetlands, prairies, mountains, tropical forests, deserts, temperate forests. And somehow species have found ways to survive in each of these very different habitats. The idea of biodiversity also includes all those ways to survive, or adaptations.

The mountain goat's woolly coat and nimble feet are wonderfully adapted for climbing over cold, rocky slopes.

The Texas horned lizard's rough body and spiny horns blend in perfectly with tree bark.

The polar bear's thick fur and fat stores help it withstand Arctic temperatures.

In the Arizona desert, the giant saguaro cactus has a thick, leafless stem that expands when it is filled with water. During the dry season, the stem folds inward in pleats, holding in water. Those features enable it to survive temperatures that soar to 50°C (120°F) and months without rainfall.

In a very different environment, deep within the ocean, sea worms swim and breathe, capturing food with feathery, fingerlike projections. They too have learned to live successfully in their home.

This variety of adaptations makes it more likely that no matter what changes take place, some forms of life will survive.

C Biodiversity means that even in the harshest regions, some species—such as the saguaro cactus—will find ways to adapt.

Cultures Have to Be Different, Too

Scientists believe that the human species evolved on the Earth somewhere in Africa more than 200,000 years ago. As the population slowly grew, people had to spread out. For most of human history, people were nomadic. They moved from place to place through the seasons, following the growth of plants and the animals they needed for food, shelter, and clothing.

Humans gradually moved farther and farther away, exploring different places. They traveled thousands of kilometers (over tens of thousands of years, of course), all on foot, and settled down in such different regions as what we now call Europe, India, and North America. They also traveled by boat to Australia and New Zealand and to the islands of the South Pacific. They learned to live in ecosystems as diverse as deserts, mountaintops, seacoasts, grasslands, and rain forests.

People on the grasslands of Europe, Asia, and the Americas learned which wild grasses they could eat and when they would be ripe. They learned to make flour by grinding the seeds of those grasses. On the coast of the Aegean Sea, between present-day Greece and Turkey, people learned how to make hooked harpoons and nets from plant fibers to catch the local fish and shellfish. They found that hollowed-out tree trunks made sturdy boats that would take them out to sea. Each group of people passed on its knowledge to the new generation.

As each group learned how to live in its environment, different cultures with different kinds of food, clothing, and shelter

The Earth's many different cultures are the human species' greatest adaptation. This Maasai hunter, Malaysian teenager, and Native American woman each belong to a culture with unique abilities and knowledge for survival.

developed. The Incas lived a rugged life high in the cold Andes Mountains in South America. They tamed wild llamas and used them to carry food supplies up and down the steep slopes. They wore warm clothing made from llama wool. In the river valleys of the Middle East, the Sumerians lived very differently. The warm climate and fertile soil gave them plenty to eat, and they wore light clothing made of woven linen. As cultures spread across the world, groups also developed different languages and beliefs.

This diversity of cultures made humans as a whole better able to adapt to changing conditions. The Sahara Desert was once a grassland with many lakes and rivers. But over thousands of years the climate became drier and drier, and people gradually moved to other places. They learned how to live in the new areas from the cultures that were already there.

Cultural variety gives us a huge pool of talents, skills, and knowledge to draw from. It is the main reason for our success as a species.

Is the Earth Alive?

Have you ever watched an anthill really closely? The famous biologist Edward O. Wilson has, and he has come up with a whole new way of thinking about anthills.

Ants are social insects—they cooperate with each other to achieve a goal. The main goal of ants is growth of the colony. To achieve this goal, ants defend their queen to the death, travel many meters to find food supplies, and carry out all the jobs needed to build a strong and secure nest. Some worker ants cut leaves, others dig the nest, and still others look after the baby ants. A large anthill might have a million ants, moving 18,000 kilograms (40,000 pounds) of soil. Long columns of ants go out from the nest like arms, doing their work of gathering leaves and finding food. If you squint your eyes and let them go out of focus, Wilson says, the busily moving anthill will look like a single animal, with different body parts each doing their job to keep the whole thing alive.

Another great scientist, James Lovelock, wondered if the Earth might work in the same way. He wondered how the Earth has stayed the same in some important ways over a long period of time. How has the amount of oxygen and carbon dioxide in the air stayed nearly the same for millions of years? Why haven't the oceans boiled away, since the sun has gotten 25 percent hotter since Earth was formed? Why haven't the oceans become saltier and saltier, since rivers and streams flowing into them are constantly bringing salts dissolved from rock and soil?

His answer was that perhaps all living things on Earth act together to keep Earth working properly. If that is true, then just like the parts of your body—eyes and heart and skin—everything on Earth has a purpose in maintaining the health and life of the whole planet.

⊂ An ant colony operates much like a single organism. Each ant does its job to further the life and growth of the whole group.

Killing Our Kin

At the beginning of this chapter, we said there were about 10 to 15 million species on Earth. But that's just one estimate. Other estimates vary from 2 million to 100 million. We really don't know how many there are. Yet some people think we can destroy nature when it suits us and then figure out how to fix anything that goes wrong.

Suppose you were hired to manage a supermarket. What's the first thing you'd do? You would probably find out what was in the store. How many departments are there? What items are sold in each department? What kind of fruit is there in the produce department? How many kinds of bread are there in the bakery department? What kinds of cheeses, meats, and salads do you have in the deli? Where do you get all these items? You would not be able to run the store unless you knew the answers to these questions.

We have nothing like that kind of information about Earth's life-forms. Biologists have identified a mere 1.5 million species. That means they've seen and put names on that many. It doesn't mean they know how many members of each species there are, what they eat, how they reproduce, or how they interact with other species. Biologists probably know that kind of detail about just a fraction of 1 percent of the species that have been identified. We couldn't manage a supermarket with so little information, so how do we think we can manage the world?

It is natural for species to flourish and then die out over time as conditions change. But scientists have identified five periods over the past 500 million years when large numbers of species rapidly became extinct. After each of these periods, or crashes, it took about 10 million years for the Earth to recover to its previous level of biodiversity. The last of these crashes happened 65 million years ago, when the dinosaurs became extinct. At least they were around for a long time—about 175 million years. Human beings have been around for less than a million years.

Now we are in a sixth extinction crisis, which is different from all the others. This time, one species alone, *Homo sapiens,* has created it. We are killing off species outright or destroying their habitats up to 10,000 times faster than ever before in Earth's history. Human activities such as clear-cutting forests, damming rivers, polluting the environment, and digging up land to build cities and farms are killing off an estimated 50,000 species in the world each year—that's 6 every hour!

Here are just two examples. Half the number of fungus species in all of Western Europe have died out in the last 60 years, mainly because of air pollution. Because many of these fungi helped trees absorb nutrients from the soil, the trees are in danger, too. There is an ecosystem along the Pacific coast of the United States that contains one-quarter of all the plant species in North America. This entire ecosystem is at serious risk of extinction because people are building on the land.

In North America more than 6000 species are estimated to be at risk. But those are just the ones we know about. Most of the species that are vanishing have never been discovered by scientists. A huge number of unknown species disappear forever when their forest, wetland, and coral reef homes are destroyed.

But there are signs of hope. Many people are trying to find ways to stop destroying land and species. Laws have been passed to control pollution from cars and factories. Seed banks have been set up to preserve the seeds of endangered food crops so that they can continue to be grown. Better methods of logging have been developed to allow trees to grow back and prevent the forest ecosystem from being destroyed. Conservation areas have been set up to keep some species alive. But we must do much more. Most important, we humans will have to realize that saving our kin in the plant and animal world means saving ourselves.

We know so little about the Earth's creatures and how they all connect. But like Noah's ark, the Earth sails through the universe carrying its vast cargo of creatures for a reason. We need our relatives—even our own personal colonies of mites and microbes.

Humpback whale

Rhinoceros

These are just four of thousands of species at risk of disappearing from the Earth.

Manatee

Siberian tiger

The Animal Canoe

This myth, told by the Ntomba people of Africa, describes how people and animals worked together to capture the Sun.

When the first people were born, in the African country of Zaire, there was no sunlight, only moonlight. In fact, the people called the moon Sun.

One day Mokele, the young son of Chief Wai, said, "Father, does the real Sun not shine here?"

"Why, what do you mean?" the chief asked.

"You will see," said Mokele. "I will go and buy the Sun for you!" And he set about to carve a beautiful canoe from the largest tree in the forest.

When it was finished, the animals of the forest came out to admire it. First came the wasps, buzzing around Mokele's head. "Let us come with you," they whispered in his ear. "If the owners won't sell you the Sun, we will sting them!"

"Good idea!" said Mokele. *"Bokendela!"* That means "Come on board!"

Just as the wasps were settled in the canoe, the turtle Nkulu crept over. "I want to come, too," he said.

Mokele laughed. "What can you do? You're too slow!"

"Too slow?" said Nkulu, offended. "I am the first one here of all the wingless creatures! Besides, I have magic powers. I can tell where the Sun is hidden."

"All right—*bokendela!*" said Mokele.

Next to arrive was the kite bird Nkombe. "I'll help you, too!" he cawed.

"And what can you do?" asked Mokele.

The kite answered, "If the owners won't let you have the Sun, I can snatch it up and fly off with it."

"Fine! Welcome aboard!" said Mokele.

Then came the leopard, the baboon, and the water buffalo. One by one, all the animals of the forest came to plead their case for going along on the journey. Mokele welcomed them all, and soon the canoe was overflowing with wild creatures.

After many days on the river, the animal canoe finally arrived at the Land of the Sun, which was ruled by the old chief Mokulaka. Mokele greeted him politely and said, "Mokulaka, I'd like to buy the Sun from you."

The chief didn't want to give up the Sun, but when he saw the canoeful of mighty animals, he knew he would have to be crafty to avoid the sale. "I will gladly let you have it," Mokulaka said, "but wait till my son Yakalaki comes to help us settle on a fair price."

Mokele agreed. Meanwhile, Mokulaka called his daughter, Molumbu. "Brew up some poison for these strangers," he told her. "I want them all killed!"

Molumbu went to carry out her father's order, without noticing that a wasp was hovering nearby. The wasp flew off to Mokele and told him what she had heard. Realizing he could not trust the chief, Mokele decided to take the Sun by force. He pretended to suspect nothing, and followed Molumbu to her hut.

Now, Mokele was very handsome, and it wasn't long before Molumbu changed her mind about the poison. She threw it onto the floor. She and Mokele decided to get married.

Meanwhile, the turtle had learned that the Sun was hidden in a cave. He set off with the kite, who grasped the Sun with his talons and lifted it high in the sky. As the brilliant rays of the Sun lit up the Earth for the first time, Mokele and the animals dashed toward their boat. Just then the chief and his son appeared with a pack of warriors and gave chase. But the wasps swooped down, stinging them so fiercely that they fell in defeat.

And so Mokele, his bride, and his animal crew returned home, where the people greeted them with loud cheers and wreaths of flowers. As the animals strolled back to their forest homes, Mokele called out to them. "Thank you, my friends!" he said. "Without the help of each one of you, there would be no Sun in the sky today. And now the world is perfect."

Love Story

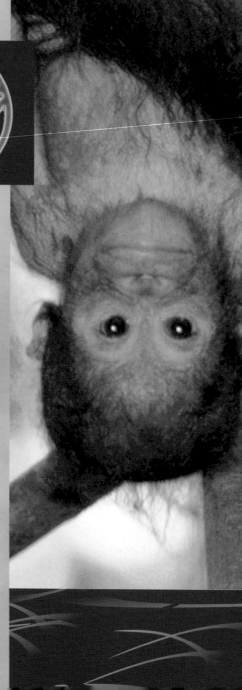

6

Most animals tenderly care for their babies. When a baby stickleback fish strays from its seaweed nest, the father will pick it up with its mouth and gently return it. Mothers often risk their own lives to protect their babies from harm. Many birds that nest on the ground try to lure intruders away from the nest by putting on an act. The killdeer cries loudly and flops about as if it had a broken wing. The purple sandpiper runs off in a zigzag pattern, its head down and wings drooping to look like back legs, all the while squeaking like a mouse. Some animals, such as the Pacific salmon, even sacrifice their lives for their young. You could say that this is "just" instinct. But this "instinct" shows that love in its many forms is part of life's plan. It may be necessary for survival.

Love Makes
You Healthy

Humans especially need to love and be loved. Like many other animals, we are born unable to look after ourselves. But we must spend a much longer time in the care of adults, growing and learning. And it's not enough just to be fed and clothed and sheltered. In order to thrive, we must also be loved.

Many studies have shown that love in the first years of life is necessary for a child to be healthy and happy and to be able to learn. When a parent loves a child, the child returns that love completely. Love makes us feel secure and teaches us how to love ourselves and others.

The world offers too many examples of what can happen when young children do not receive love. In Croatia, in Eastern Europe, wars have separated thousands of children from their families. One group of children, who were about six years old and just starting school, had many problems. They did not want to eat, had nightmares, threw tantrums, and felt sad all the time. Without the love and protection of adults close to them, these children faced an unhappy future.

But when these orphans were adopted by new parents who gave them the love they needed, many of them changed miraculously. Their problems went away, and they were soon laughing and playing and making friends. Others kids slowly began to feel better but still had some problems. And a few unlucky children didn't get better at all.

The need for love never goes away. It seems that as we need air and water and food, we need also to give and receive love, right to the end of our lives.

Even Cells Need Love

Many forms of life are attracted to each other—even cells. All plants and animals are clumps of microscopic cells. You probably have about 45 trillion of them in your body. Cells come in many shapes and sizes, depending on what they do in the body and what kind of body they are in.

Scientists who study cells have discovered that when two cells are brought close together, the thin walls that separate them tend to fuse, and the jelly-like cytoplasm inside the two cells flows together. You could say that cells are attracted to each other.

Many kinds of animals, such as monkeys, wolves, and bees, are attracted to each other, too. They are social beings that like to live in groups. Many animals clearly show their attraction to each other. When coyotes choose their mates, for example, they celebrate with a long, joyful duet of howling. Even plants seem to like to be together. Often a houseplant with droopy leaves will perk up when it is placed with other plants.

Different kinds of molecules often bond together to form new substances. Water, for instance, is made up of hydrogen and oxygen molecules bound together. In fact, all matter is attracted to all other matter. It's the way the universe works.

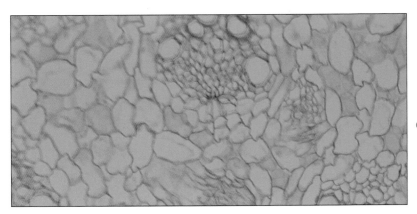

⊂ Mutual attraction, or love, is built into life at every level—from animals to plant cells like these, right down to molecules and atoms.

You Need Family, Friends, and Neighbors

What's the best thing about school? Homework? More likely it's being with your friends. We humans, like many animals, are very social beings. We need love and security, and the place to find them is in families and communities. When we're part of a group of people who share the same values and who value each other, we feel safe. We feel that we belong.

For 99 percent of the time that humans have been on Earth, we lived in small tribal groups that moved from place to place. Within these groups our ancestors learned to hunt and gather food, fought off predators, found mates, and shared stories, music, and rituals. The most important consideration in making decisions was the survival and well-being of the group.

Then, about 10,000 years ago, people discovered how to grow their own plants, such as wheat and beans. They also learned how to tame wild animals, such as goats and sheep, and raise them for food. This was the beginning of agriculture. To take care of crops, people had to settle down in one place.

Soon farm communities developed, and eventually some of these grew into villages and towns. This was a huge change in a pattern of life that had lasted tens of thousands of years. When people began to live in large towns and cities, they no longer knew their neighbors but lived among strangers.

In North America, a change from country to city living has taken place very rapidly. In just the last 150 years, people also had to get used to more and more technological advances, from airplanes to computers. It's not surprising that many people today feel lonely and cut off from a supporting group.

ONCE WE WERE HUNTERS

Years ago

300,000–200,000 First humans, *Homo sapiens,* appear in Africa. A similar people, the Neanderthals, appears in Europe and Asia. Both groups live by hunting and by gathering wild grains and fruits. They make stone tools.

40,000 *Homo sapiens* now the dominant species. They have spread throughout Europe, the Middle East, Asia, and Australia.

30,000 People gradually cross over to North America from Asia. They can travel by foot, since the two continents are joined at this time. The hunters follow huge herds of wild bison, reindeer, mammoths, and horses. From there people begin to spread southward through North America. People have now reached Australia.

28,000 Last Neanderthals disappear.

13,000 People now living in Central and South America.

10,000 Farming begins in Middle East. People learn how to plant grains, such as wheat, and to herd wild goats and sheep. First permanent settlements form.

9000 Corn is grown in Mexico. Farming takes place in Africa.

8000 Farming villages develop in China and South America. People in western Europe herd sheep and goats, and later plant grains.

6500 Farming develops in India and in central and northern Europe.

6000 Horses tamed in Russia. Cattle herded in Africa.

5000 Farming villages develop in Peru. Llamas tamed and used for wool and meat and for carrying loads.

5500 First cities built in the fertile river valleys of Sumeria (present-day Iraq).

For most of the time that humans have been on Earth, we lived in small family and tribal groups as hunter-gatherers. These dates are based on discoveries made so far about the distant past, before any written records were kept. The names of places are what we call them now—we don't know what people of the time called them.

Why Dogs (and Trees) Are Our Best Friends

Do you have a pet? If you do, you know the strong bond we humans can have with other animals—even a bird, fish, or turtle. That's love. Or maybe you know the delight of tending a garden and seeing it grow from tiny seeds into plump red tomatoes, crunchy green beans, or glorious golden sunflowers. That's a kind of love, too.

Those feelings give you a hint of the connection that humans had with the natural world for thousands of years. Through most of our species' history, the wild creatures around us were companions, not just sources of food.

We believe that our first ancestors lived in Africa. They were surrounded by a huge array of creatures. People listened to the animals' calls at night. They saw the sky come alive with winged creatures, the trees dance with movement, the plains thunder with hoofbeats. These living beings were much more than a background to human activity—they were part of the show.

Because of our long history living with other creatures, some scientists believe that humans may have developed a need to be in the company of other beings. We seem to have an emotional bond with other living things—love for them. It's another kind of love that's part of who we were. Or should be.

⊂ Dogs were the first wild animals our ancestors tamed. They have been our companions and loving friends for 80,000 years.

BeYond Awesome

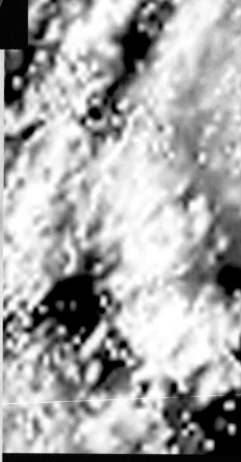

7

Where did we come from? Why are we here? What happens to us after we die?

Have you ever asked yourself those questions? If so, you're like most of the people who ever lived on Earth. From the earliest times people have tried to answer these questions through stories and myths.

There are thousands of these stories. According to different versions, humans were shaped out of clay and water, carved from twigs, or hatched from a huge egg. Most of these creation myths start with the same idea—humans were made from the Earth's elements, just as science says we were.

Creation stories were considered the most sacred of all stories. They gave shape to the world people lived in. They gave them rules to live by. And they gave them reasons for the cruelties and misfortunes of life. Humans had qualities that other animals did not, such as greed, pride, and ambition. People knew these qualities caused much of the grief in the world and wanted explanations for them.

Most of our stories tell about a time when humans disobeyed their gods, tried to be gods themselves, and were punished for it. In the Prometheus myth, Pandora opens the forbidden box and lets loose a rain of evils on the world. In the story of the Garden of Eden, Adam and Eve eat the apple from the tree of knowledge, and for their disobedience they are banished from the garden.

Blame It on the Brain

Humans are curious animals with a drive to learn more and more about their world. This curiosity comes from our brain. We humans have a large and complex brain. It has given us not only curiosity but also consciousness, memory, and the ability to plan ahead. We can learn from experience, and unlike other animals, we can pass on our knowledge to the next generation. For this reason, we have evolved much faster than ordinary evolution would have allowed.

But consciousness has also given us the sorrowful knowledge that we will die. We need our stories to help us accept this greatest mystery of all. All cultures have believed in a power greater than human power, in some kind of life after death, and in something within us that is eternal—our soul or spirit.

IT'S ALL IN YOUR HEAD

Our brain gives us consciousness, memory, and the ability to plan ahead. This brain map shows areas of the brain that control different body functions.

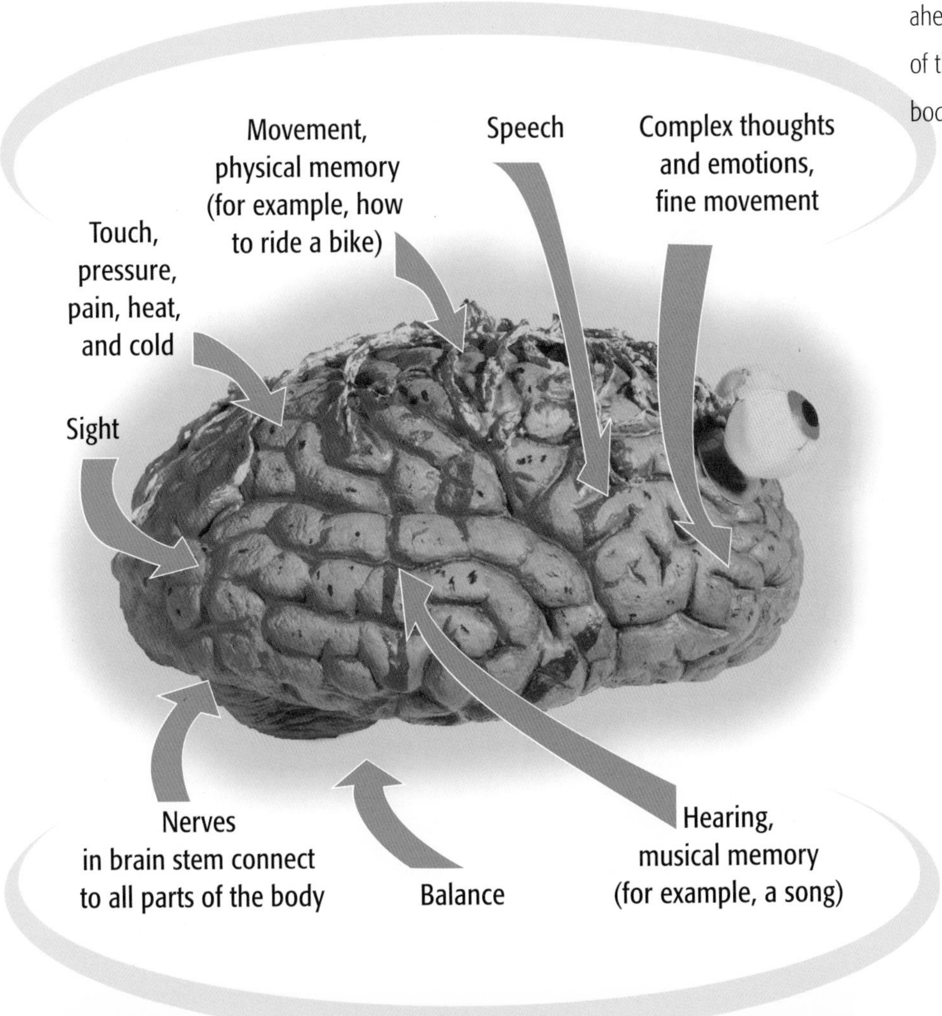

Touch, pressure, pain, heat, and cold

Movement, physical memory (for example, how to ride a bike)

Speech

Complex thoughts and emotions, fine movement

Sight

Nerves in brain stem connect to all parts of the body

Balance

Hearing, musical memory (for example, a song)

Memories are stored in different parts of the brain

The Gifts of Spider Woman

Here is a creation story told by the Hopi people.

The Hopi people believed that the great god of the universe, Sotuknang, commanded his helper–goddess, Spider Woman, to create the first people. When she had done this, she took a long look at her handiwork. She decided that some finishing touches were needed. She said to Sotuknang: "As you have commanded me I have created these First People. They are fully and firmly formed; they are properly colored; they have life; they have movement. But they cannot talk. That is the proper thing they lack. So I want you to give them speech. Also the wisdom and power to reproduce, so that they may enjoy their life, and give thanks to the Creator."

Different Cultures Have Different Pictures of the World

Traditional cultures today, like our earliest ancestors, see the world in a very different way from modern cultures. To people in traditional cultures—such as the Aborigines in Australia, the Yanomami people in Brazil, or the Haida people on the west coast of Canada—everything is alive with spirit. The mountains, forests, rivers, winds, and lakes are ruled by gods. Each tree, stone, or animal may have a soul like ours. And the spirits of the dead and yet-to-be-born may be present around us. People are just one part of this grand symphony of souls. One of our responsibilities in keeping the universe working as it should is to carry out various rituals and sacred ceremonies.

The Aborigines in Australia, for instance, tell a beautiful story about how the world began. They say that the Ancestors sang it into existence. The people's role is to keep the Earth sacred by continuing to sing the ancient songs, which have been handed down through the generations. They believe that their land is sacred and that each part of it has a spirit. Sometimes one of the spirits will decide to take on human form for a while, and that's how people are born. Each person, then, is truly joined with the Earth and will suffer and die if he or she wanders too far from home.

This feeling of being part of a spirit-filled world is very different from the way most modern people feel today. Instead, many of us see ourselves as separate from our environment. You are you, and the rest of the world is outside you. When you look

We have to feel the heartbeats of the trees, because trees are living beings like us.

—Sunderlal Bahuguna, spokesperson for the Chipko Movement

at a tree, you know it isn't a part of you, right? And it certainly doesn't have a soul. We take that idea for granted, without even thinking about it.

At some point in history we lost our feeling of spiritual connection to the rest of the world. We stopped seeing a spirit in the tree and began taking the tree's measurements. (Let's see, it's so many meters high, its leaves are shaped in such-and-such a way, and we can get so much money for it if we cut it down.) The tree was no longer our kin but something completely different from us. As we lost that connection, we also began to make bigger and bigger changes to our world.

And so we have created our own universe, filled with office buildings and cars and sports stadiums and shopping malls and all the other things that can seem much more real and important than rivers and birds. Our human-made world doesn't have spirits in it—it has things. But this is a lonely way to live. Separated from the spirits of the Earth, we are strangers in our own home.

Some Things Are Sacred

Think about your room at home. Has anyone ever said, "This room is a mess! You don't need all that junk"? But to you, it's probably a great room, and you don't want to part with a thing. You'd never give up your catcher's mitt, a present from your dad. And you certainly need your books—you can remember reading every one, or having them read to you, for the first time. Last year's Halloween space-monster costume has to stay. It's so cool, and besides, you made it. How about that beat-up old teddy bear you had when you were small? Or those seashells you got five summers ago at your grandma's? Nope. Everything in your room is part of what makes it special to you. Even the really old things are important, because they bring back memories you want to keep in your mind and heart.

Not everybody would think that the things in your room are valuable, but they mean a lot to you. They have a kind of spiritual value. Spiritual values have to do with feelings and memories. They have nothing to do with money. They are priceless.

Native people believe that nature has deep spiritual value. Many other people, including scientists, agree. A walk through the forest or in a meadow scattered with wildflowers refreshes our spirits and connects us with Earth. It is a sacred place.

An American author named Robert Jay Lifton once told an amazing story about what happened after the bombing of Hiroshima, a city in Japan, at the end of World War II. The atomic bomb had destroyed the city and killed about 100,000 people. The blast had also sent a cloud of deadly atomic rays across the city, causing a terrible sickness. Afterward, a rumor spread that nothing would ever grow on that ground again. And this possibility was a greater horror to the people than all the deaths and destruction caused by the bomb itself. Only after grass began to grow again did people start to feel better.

People need to know that nature will continue. Without thinking about it, we count on the sounds of birds and crickets, the ebb and flow of the tides, the blossoming of trees every spring. It could be that spiritual connection to creation is another of our absolute needs, just like air, water, earth, fire, our plant and animal kin, and love.

It's Your World Now

8

You will spend most of your life in the 21st century. This will be your world, and unfortunately it's in pretty bad shape. Pollution, destruction of ecosystems, global warming, ozone holes, extinction of species—these are huge problems that require huge efforts from countries all over the world. But countries are made up of individuals, and each one can do something to help.

"But I'm Only a Kid—
I Can't Change the World"

Young people often know more about what's happening to the environment than older people do. And many of them are working hard to change things. The following stories are just three examples to show what kids and teenagers can do.

↺ Craig Keilburger and African friends.

Free The Children

Craig Kielburger, now 16, is a Toronto student and founder of Free the Children, an international organization that works to find alternatives to child labor. In some countries, children may work long hours in factories or shops for very little money. Here is how Craig got started.

I first learned that children have the power to help the world when I was 7 years old. My older brother, Marc, was 13 at the time. He had discovered that many of the cleaning products we use every day in our homes contain dangerous chemicals that end up in drains and waterways, harming plant and animal life. Marc did a series of experiments to prove that safe alternative cleaners could be just as effective. He organized a petition for the government to pass a law requiring the labeling of cleaning products to protect our waterways.

Marc was my hero! I loved to listen to him practice the speeches that he gave at schools to convince other kids to start environment clubs and take action in their neighborhoods. Sometimes, when Marc and his friends visited high schools to get names on his petition, he would invite me along to help gather signatures. He didn't have to tell me what to say, because I had listened to him so many times speak about how everything we do in life has a good or bad effect on the world.

My friends and I were 12 years old when we started the organization called Free the Children. We wanted not only to help free children from the exploitation and abuse of child labor but also to free kids from the idea that they are not old enough or smart enough or capable enough to help others and change the world. In the past three years, the young people from Free the Children have spoken to teachers, business people, and world leaders about children's rights. They have organized petitions and letter-writing campaigns. Children have raised funds to open 12 schools in the developing world and have put together many thousands of school and health kits to help their peers. They have bought cows and sewing machines as alternatives sources of income for families so they can send their children to school rather than work. They have bought land for families to grow their own food so that their children could stop begging on the streets.

There is an African proverb that says that it takes a village to raise a child. We believe that it also takes a child to help raise a village! I think that kids are the ones who will change the world.

ORCA FIGHTS FOR THE TAILED FROGS

ORCA is a group of 20 West Vancouver children and their families who get together regularly to study nature, learn outdoor skills, and take on projects to help the environment. These projects have included banding birds, cleaning up beaches, and building a butterfly garden. But the most exciting project for four ORCA kids was helping a researcher at the University of British Columbia search local streams for a rare species called the tailed frog. That trip turned into a bigger adventure than they'd expected.

I was with the group when we happened to stumble upon the tailed frog tadpoles. Unfortunately, where we found them was in a creek in a major development area. We had to stop this. The developer was asking city council for permission to develop there. Four of us decided to go to council and ask for bigger areas of space around the creek. After quite a few meetings with the council and the developer, they finally gave some space for the frogs. This goes to show that if kids try hard enough they can make a difference.

—Tristan Huntington, age 12

We fought hard for the tailed frogs because they couldn't speak for themselves. I really believe that to have such interesting animals in our community says a lot about the wonderful place we live. Unfortunately if we were to lose this animal after all we know, it would say even more. We should all try not to lose anything from nature.

—David Meszaros, age 11

The tailed frog experience was rewarding because it elevated the level of environmental awareness in both kids and adults. It just goes to show that in order to achieve something, it takes conviction and perseverance. If you knock loud enough and long enough at the gate, someone is bound to hear you.

–Kathleen Fawley, age 12

The four of us kids going to city council was a great experience–not because of the media but because I know I have made a difference in the world.

–Michael VanInsberghe, age 11

By spring 1999, all creeks in West Vancouver were being monitored for tailed frogs. Also, wider buffer zones around the creeks were being established, tree cutting in the area was restricted, and special filters had been attached to storm drains leading into the creeks. Most important, the ORCA kids' efforts to save the frogs had made people in the community much more aware of the need to protect species and habitats.

↺ Members of ORCA being filmed.

BRINGING BACK THE PEREGRINE FALCON

Grade 11 student Lauren Telford worked on the Return of the Peregrine Falcon Project. Here, she describes her experience:

In February 1998, an environmental biologist visited our high school with Arthur, his live peregrine falcon. His impassioned awareness of this beautiful species' struggle to survive struck a sympathetic chord in me. The presentation finished with information about the Return of the Peregrine Falcon Project. It would attempt to bring back this extirpated [extinct in this area] species to the Okanagan Valley [in British Columbia]. I immediately applied to help with the project.

A month later, eight other teenagers and I became the project's student spokespersons. We traveled to schools in the Okanagan with a falconer and a B.C. senior naturalist, talking to children about how they could play a part in saving endangered species. One way we did this was with an art contest. The winning pieces were made into an endangered wildlife greeting card set. Not only do they inform us of the decreasing population of natural wildlife but are proof that children too can make a difference.

That summer, I traveled back and forth among four community libraries, teaching children aged 4 to 13 about endangered species and endangered spaces. Using resources at the libraries—people, books, and the Internet—I created my own education programs.

I invented games and activities, told stories, and showed movie clips to illustrate weekly themes, each focusing on different endangered animals or spaces. I had no prior experience teaching, so I had to teach myself as I went along.

I've participated in many voluntary activities, but none has affected me more than the Return of the Peregrine Falcon Project. Working for both the long- and short-term goals of this project has been a journey of discovery.

Members of the Return of the Peregrine Falcon Project released nine young falcons in 1998. They later received reports that seven had migrated successfully to Guatemala. The workers hoped that at least two birds would make it back to Canada in the summer of 1999. They planned to release twelve more fledglings that year. Once a species is gone from an area, it takes a long time to bring it back.

First, Clean Up the Backyard

You might wonder, how do I get started? Here are some simple things you can do for the Earth—and yourself.

- Talk to your parents and grandparents. Ask them what it was like when they were kids. What kind of animals and plants did they see? Do they remember forests or fields that have disappeared since then? How did that happen? Tell them what you know about damage to the environment. Talk about what you can all do to help repair it.

- Find out how ordinary things work—such as sewage, garbage, water, electricity, food, clothing. Where do they start? What happens to them? Where do they go?

- At home and at school, practice the three *R's:* Reduce, Reuse, Recycle—especially Reduce. That means buying and using less.

- Ask yourself before buying something: Do I really need this?

- Walk, bike, or Rollerblade as much as possible, rather than asking someone to drive you.

- Plant trees.

- Check out environmental groups in your area and consider volunteering.

- Get out into nature whenever you can. And when you get there—let it amaze you!

Lifting Up the Sky

The Snohomish people tell this story.

When the Creator made the world, he started in the east. Then he moved slowly westward. In a big sack he carried many languages, and as he went along creating tribes of people here and there, he gave each one a language. When he came to Puget Sound, in the state of Washington, he liked it so much he decided to stop there. But he still had a lot of languages in his sack, so he scattered them all around the area. That's why there are so many Native languages in the Puget Sound region.

Because they spoke so many different languages, the people couldn't talk to each other. But it turned out that all of them agreed on one thing—the Creator had made the sky much too low. Tall people were always bumping their heads on it. And sometimes people would do something they were forbidden to do. They would climb up into the tall trees and enter the Sky World.

Finally, the wisest elders of all the tribes had a meeting to see what could be done about the sky. They decided they would have to try to push it up. But how could they do that?

"We can do it if we get together and push at the same time," said one elder. "We will need all the people and the animals and the birds."

"But how will we know when to push?" asked another elder. "We speak so many different languages. How can we get everyone to push together?"

The elders thought about this for a while. Finally, one of the elders said, "Why don't we use a signal? When we have everything ready and it is time to push, one of us can shout *"Ya-hoh."* That means `Lift together' in all our languages." And so it was agreed.

The wise men went back to their villages and spread the word about the sky-lifting attempt. They told the people and the animals and the birds where and on what day the event would take place and what the signal would be to push together. Then everyone got busy making poles from the tallest pine trees, to be used in pushing against the sky.

When the big day came, everyone gathered at the chosen spot. The people and animals lifted their poles till they touched the sky. Then, when the wise men shouted *"Ya-hoh!"* they all pushed as hard as they could. The sky moved a couple of centimeters (an inch). On the second *"Ya-hoh!"* everyone again pushed, and the sky moved up just a bit more. Again the signal was given, and again the assembled group pushed with all its might.

All day the signal rang out, and each time the people pushed until their muscles ached and the sweat ran down their bodies. At last they gave one last mighty heave, and the sky moved up to where it is now. Since then, people and animals have walked around freely without bumping their heads against the sky, and no one has been able to enter the Sky World. And the Snohomish people still say *"Ya-hoh!"* when they are doing hard work or lifting something heavy such as a canoe. When they hear this signal, they use every bit of their strength to accomplish the task together.

THE CALL OF THE MALL

Are you a mall rat? If so, you're not alone—93 percent of American girls say that store-hopping is their favorite activity. It can be fun to buy a great new outfit or the latest CD. But is that the only thing that's fun or has any value? For many people, it seems that it is. Buying more and more objects is a major way people today look for happiness and purpose in life. Look at these facts:

- Toy makers produce up to 6000 new toys each year. (That's on top of the old toys already for sale.)

- Americans spend an average of 6 hours a week shopping. They spend just 40 minutes a week playing with their children.

- We can choose from more than 11,000 magazines and 25,000 supermarket items, including 200 kinds of cereal.

- North Americans will spend an average of two years of their lives just watching TV commercials.

But owning things by itself doesn't seem to make people happy. Buying something makes you feel happy for a little while. Then you have to buy something else to feel happy again. Meanwhile, all this shopping is eating up the Earth. Many natural resources, such as oil, trees, and aluminum, are used to make, advertise, and sell all those things we buy. Added to that is the waste these purchases create—the bags and boxes they come in, the advertising flyers, and the things themselves when we throw them away. This mountain of garbage gets burned in incinerators, dumped into lakes, or buried in the ground, where it contaminates the air, water, and soil.

- In the last 60 years, Americans alone have used up as large a share of the Earth's mineral resources as all people in the world used before that time.

- In the last 200 years, the United States has lost 85 percent of its old-growth forests, 50 percent of its wetlands, and 99 percent of its tallgrass prairies.

Get the connection?

Trust In Nature

Nature has a remarkable ability to heal itself, given half a chance. Fish returned to the River Thames in England after anti-pollution laws were passed, and plants started growing again around Sudbury, Ontario, after metal-making factories installed scrubbers, which cut down on the toxic gases going into the air.

This new century could bring about bigger miracles. But we humans must be creative and generous and strong enough to make that happen. Some people say that protecting the environment costs too much. They say there are more important things than grizzly bears and prairies and rivers. But what can be more important than this precious home we share?

The Earth has sailed through the universe for billions of years, slowly creating the perfect conditions for life in all its fabulous variety. We don't know how that works. We can't control the tides or the seasons. We can't create a tropical forest and fill it with hundreds of thousands of species all working together to keep it healthy. Only nature can do these things. All we can do is try to let nature keep on doing them.

Our survival depends on remembering who we are. We are the Earth—part of the air, water, soil, and energy of the world; beings with love in our hearts, life in our souls, and a kingdom of kin at our doorstep. It is up to us to protect those things so that they will be around for many generations to come.

⌒ We must protect the Earth, for we *are* the Earth.

GLOSSARY

aboriginal   Having to do with the people who have inhabited a land since the earliest times—for example, Native Canadians and Americans and Australian Aborigines.

air sacs   Tiny balloon-like pouches in the lungs that let oxygen pass into the blood vessels and let carbon dioxide pass out.

argon   One of the less plentiful gases in the Earth's atmosphere. Argon makes up only about 1 percent of the atmosphere.

atmosphere   The air surrounding the Earth.

atom   The smallest particle of matter.

biodiversity   The variety of plants, animals, and ecosystems in the world.

bronchi   Tubes in the lungs that branch out like tree branches from the windpipe. Singular is *bronchus*.

bronchioles   Smaller tubes that branch out from the bronchi.

carbohydrates   A group of substances in food that supply energy. Some foods that have a lot of carbohydrates in them are vegetables, fruit, and bread.

carbon dioxide   A gas that animals breathe out into the air and that plants take in from the air.

cell   The basic unit of life. Each cell is enclosed by a membrane that separates it from other cells.

coal   A hard black rock that formed over millions of years from plant remains. Coal is used as a fuel.

condensation   The changing of a gas into a liquid. For example, water vapor (a gas) condenses into clouds and may fall as rain (a liquid).

developed country   A country that is relatively rich, with many industries and technological advances—for example, Canada, the United States, France, and Japan.

developing country A country that is beginning to have more industries and technological advances but is still relatively poor—for example, Kenya, Guatemala, and Thailand.

ecosystem A community of interacting animals and plants and their environment.

energy The ability to do work. Energy is never created or lost but only changed from one form to another.

esophagus A tube through which food passes from the mouth to the stomach.

evaporation The changing of a liquid into a gas. For example, water (a liquid) changes into water vapor (a gas) when you boil it.

extinct species A species of animal or plant that no longer exists in the world; all members of the species have died. The dinosaur *Tyrannosaurus rex* is an example of an extinct species.

fossil fuel A natural fuel such as coal or gas formed in the Earth billions of years ago from the remains of animals and plants.

fungi A group of organisms that are similar to plants but do not have chlorophyll and reproduce by means of spores rather than seeds. Mushrooms, toadstools, yeast, and mold are examples of fungi. Singular is *fungus.*

gas A usually invisible substance that does not have shape or volume. Water vapor (steam) is an example of a gas.

genes The material in cells that is passed on from generation to generation. These "blueprints" of life tell cells how to carry out the bodily processes that make life possible. Genes also determine features such as color of eyes and hair, height, and whether you're right- or left-handed.

gravity The force that pulls objects toward the Earth. For example, if you drop a pencil, gravity will make it fall to the floor rather than float in the air or fly up.

habitat A natural area where particular plants or animals live. A river, for example, might be the habitat of several species of fish, insects, mammals, and plants.

homeothermic Having the same body temperature all the time, no matter how hot or cold it is outside.

hydrogen The lightest gas in the atmosphere. Water molecules are made up of hydrogen and oxygen atoms.

metabolism The sum of the processes in an organism that create energy and growth.

micro-organism A plant or animal that is so small it can only be seen by looking through a microscope.

microscopic Very small; can only be seen through a microscope.

mineral A natural solid material. It is not formed from animals or plants. Salt, stone, and iron are examples of minerals.

molecule A group of atoms. For example, the water molecule is made up of two hydrogen atoms and one oxygen atom.

myth A traditional story, usually about gods, ancestors, or heroes, that explains the beliefs and values of a culture.

natural gas Gas that formed over millions of years from the remains of plants and animals and was trapped beneath the Earth's crust. Natural gas is used as a fuel.

nutrient A substance in food that is necessary for life. Fats, carbohydrates, proteins, vitamins, and minerals are examples of nutrients.

oil A thick liquid that formed over millions of years from the remains of plants and animals and was trapped beneath the Earth's crust. Oil is used mainly as a fuel.

olfactory bulb A small patch of cells high up inside the nose that picks up smells in the air we breathe in and sends messages about them to the brain.

organic Coming from plants or animals.

organism A living plant or animal.

oxygen The most important gas in the air; the element that all animals and plants need to live.

ozone layer A thin layer in the atmosphere surrounding the Earth that shields us from most of the sun's ultraviolet light rays.

photo-synthesis The process by which green plants take in carbon dioxide and water and, using sunlight, make food and release oxygen.

pituitary gland A small gland at the bottom of the brain that releases substances that are essential for growth and various body processes.

pollutant A substance that doesn't normally belong somewhere and upsets the surroundings.

proteins A group of molecules in food that are needed for health and life. Some foods that are good sources of proteins are meat, eggs, and nuts.

radiation The sending out of rays of light or heat.

species A group of plants or animals that share certain characteristics and can reproduce with each other. The horse and the human being are examples of species.

traditional culture A group of people whose values, beliefs, and practices have been handed down from generation to generation.

troposphere The lowest layer of the atmosphere, in which living things exist and weather takes place.

ultraviolet light Light rays from the sun that can be harmful to living things.

water cycle The constant circulation of water through the Earth and living things. Water vapor condenses in clouds and falls to Earth as rain or snow; collects in soil, water, and organisms; and is released back into the air through breath, sweat, and evaporation.

weathering The breaking down of rocks and other materials by forces such as wind, rain, and ice.

DO YOU REMEMBER?

Questions

1. What essential gas makes up about 21 percent of our atmosphere?

2. We breathe in carbon dioxide and breathe out oxygen. True or false?

3. Plants take in carbon dioxide and release oxygen into the air in a process called _____.

4. How does the oxygen you breathe into your lungs reach your bloodstream?

5. The layer of air in which we live and where weather happens is the _____.

6. What is the ozone layer, and why do we need it?

7. Where is most of your body's water located?

8. How much water do you need each day?

9. You need water because:
   ❏ (a) it tastes good
   ❏ (b) it contains carbohydrates
   ❏ (c) it cures warts and other skin diseases
   ❏ (d) it helps your heart keep pumping
   (Check the right answers.)

10. A molecule of sweat off your body might turn up later in (check the right answers):
    ❏ (a) a tree
    ❏ (b) a cloud
    ❏ (c) someone else's body
    ❏ (d) the ocean

11. The Earth's water cycle changes salty water into _____.

12. Which of the following are good ways to use less water during the day? (Check the right answers.)
    ❏ (a) When you're brushing your teeth, use a glass of water instead of letting the tap run the whole time.
    ❏ (b) Drink less water.
    ❏ (c) Have a quick shower rather than a bath, especially if your shower has a water-saving shower head.
    ❏ (d) If you notice a tap leaking at home or school, report it to an adult in charge of fixing it.

13. All your food comes from the soil. True or false?

14. What are the main nutrients in food that you need to be healthy?

15. Wind, rain, and ice break down rocks into small bits in a process called _____.

16. What organisms might you find in the soil?

17. How do plants and animals enrich the soil?

18. How can farmers make the soil healthier? (Check all the right answers.)
    ❏ (a) Use chemical fertilizers.
    ❏ (b) Use powerful chemical pesticides to kill every bug and weed.
    ❏ (c) Plant a variety of crops.
    ❏ (d) Right after harvesting one crop, plant another one.

19. Most people in the world eat mainly _____.

20. Where does all the energy that makes life possible come from?

21. What part of your body stays the same temperature all the time?

22. What did our early ancestors learn to do that allowed them to travel all over the world, even to cold regions?

23. Why are coal, oil, and gas called fossil fuels?

24. What are the three main ways your body keeps your inner core warm?

25. What are three ways you could use less energy during the day?

26. You provide a _____ for about six billion microscopic creatures.

27. The Earth has 10 to 15 million _____ of plants and animals.

28. How do salmon help the trees in the forest?

29. We should try to protect the many different species of plants and animals in the world (biodiversity) because (check all the right answers):
   ❏ (a) all species are connected through their life cycles
   ❏ (b) biodiversity helps species survive when conditions change
   ❏ (c) biodiversity makes our lives more beautiful and interesting

30. Why is it important to protect whole ecosystems and not just individual plant and animal species?

31. What is an extinction crisis?

32. What is causing our present extinction crisis?

33. What happens when two cells are brought close together?

34. What are social animals?

35. Besides food and shelter, what do babies need to grow and be healthy?

36. Why have people throughout history told creation stories?

37. What do we humans have that makes us most different from other animals?

38. Traditional cultures believe that _____ inhabit trees, rocks, and rivers.

39. Which of these things do humans need to live and be healthy? (Check all the right answers.)
   ❏ (a) Air
   ❏ (b) More parking lots and fewer trees
   ❏ (c) Water
   ❏ (d) The sun's energy
   ❏ (e) Shopping
   ❏ (f) Soil

40. What are "three R's" you can do to help the environment?

41. What are three other things you can do to help take care of the Earth?

Answers

1. Oxygen

2. False. We do the opposite—we breathe in oxygen and breathe out carbon dioxide.

3. Photosynthesis

4. Oxygen passes into the bloodstream through the walls of the air sacs.

5. Troposphere

6. The ozone layer is a thin layer in the Earth's atmosphere that lies above the troposphere. It shields the Earth from much of the sun's harmful ultraviolet light rays.

7. Inside your body cells

8. About 2.5 liters (quarts)—that's about 10 glasses. Some of the water, though, comes from your food.

9. (d) Water is necessary for all your body processes, such as digesting food, breathing, and circulating blood. As for the other answers, good taste is a plus but not a necessity for life. Water does not contain carbohydrates, and it won't cure warts. (If you're healthy, though, your body has a better chance of fighting off all kinds of diseases.)

10. All are possible, because they're all part of the Earth's water cycle.

11. Fresh water

12. (a), (c), and (d) are all good ways. But don't try to save water by drinking less than you need. The idea is to stop wasting water. You might be surprised how easy it is to waste water. For example, a tap that leaks only one drop per second wastes more than 25 liters (quarts) of water a day!

13. True

14. Fats, carbohydrates, proteins, and certain vitamins and minerals. You also need water and fiber.

15. Weathering

16. Worms, beetles, ants, fungi, nematodes, springtails, and bacteria are only some of the many organisms you might find in the soil. Of course, you would need a microscope to see some of them.

17. Plants and animals contain nutrients. When they die, their bodies supply the soil with these nutrients, which new plants need to grow.

18. (c) is one way to keep soil healthy. The other answers are more likely to make the soil less healthy. Using chemical fertilizers and pesticides can pollute the soil, air, and nearby

water. And planting one crop right after harvesting another crop doesn't allow soil long enough between plantings to enrich itself.

19. Grains, such as rice, wheat, and corn

20. The sun

21. The inner core. Unless you're sick, the temperature of your inner core will always stay very close to 37 °C (98 °F).

22. They learned how to control fire.

23. Because like fossils, they were formed from the remains of ancient plants and animals.

24. Metabolism, absorbing heat from the outside through your skin, and using energy from muscular movement, including shivering.

25. Some of the many ways you can use less energy are turning out lights when you're not using them, using energy-saving light bulbs, turning down the thermostat at night, recycling as much garbage as possible, and not buying things you don't need.

26. Habitat

27. Species

28. Salmon are food for animals such as bears, wolves, and eagles. After these animals have digested the salmon, they drop their feces in the forest. The droppings contain nutrients from the salmon. These nutrients go into the soil and help plants (such as trees) and animals grow.

29. (a) and (b) are necessary reasons; (c) may not be necessary, but it's a good reason too.

30. Plants and animals interact with each other and with the air, soil, and water that are part of ecosystems. They depend on all these things to survive.

31. A time when many species are becoming extinct very rapidly

32. Human beings and their activities

33. They fuse (their contents mix).

34. Animals that live in groups

35. Love

36. Some of the reasons people tell creation stores are to tell them where they came from, to tell them why they were born, to teach them good ways to behave and live, to explain why there is cruelty and misfortune in the world, to explain what happens when they die.

37. A bigger brain

38. Spirits

39. (a), (c), (d), and (f)

40. Reduce, Recycle, Reuse

41. See the list on page 105.

FUN THINGS TO DO

Get the Angle on Summer

What makes summer hot and winter cold? Try this activity to see if you can figure it out. Choose a bright summer day without much wind. Take your sun readers outside in the morning or afternoon, when the sun isn't right overhead. And don't forget—never look directly at the sun!

What you need

2 sheets of black construction paper
2 pieces of heavy cardboard or plywood
Bricks or blocks to prop up the board
Masking tape
2 thermometers

What to do

1. Cut a slit about 2.5 centimeters (1 inch) wide in the middle of each piece of paper. Tape each piece of paper to a piece of cardboard or plywood. Place a thermometer in each slit. Make sure the bulb is inside the slit and the rest of the thermometer is outside so that you can read the scale. Tape the thermometers in place.

2. Put your two sun readers outside in the shade for a few minutes until they read the same temperature. Then move them into the sunlight. Prop one board up facing the sun, tilted so that the sun's rays hit it straight on (at a perpendicular angle). Lay the other board flat on the ground, or even tilt it backward slightly, so that the rays hit it at a flat (parallel) angle.

3. Record the two temperatures every minute or so until they stop climbing. Record the final temperatures. Which temperature rose more quickly? Why?

Here's the story

As the Earth takes its yearly turn around the sun, in the Northern Hemisphere, the North Pole tilts toward the sun in the summer and away from the sun in the winter. In the Southern Hemisphere, the South Pole tilts toward the sun in the summer and away from the sun in the winter. In this activity, one board was like the Earth in summer—tilted toward the sun. The other board was like the Earth in winter—tilted away from the direct rays. When the sun's light rays hit straight on, they are concentrated and cause higher temperatures. When the light rays hit the Earth at a flatter angle, they "spread out," causing lower temperatures. It's the Earth's tilt that makes summer hot and winter cold. Notice too that the sun's light energy changes to heat energy when it reaches the Earth's air, soil, trees, and you.

Myth Making

You have read several myths and stories in this book. They come from many different cultures, but they have certain things in common. What are some of those things? Write them down and think about them. Now create your own myth. It might be about how the world began. Or it might be about where just one part of the world—bees or snakes or the wind—came from. You'll probably include some interesting animals, people, or both who have a problem to solve. You might want to add a few strange details or surprising events.

It might be fun to get some of your friends together and write a group myth. You can do this by talking over your ideas and deciding which to include in the story. Or one person can write down the beginning of the story and hand the paper to the next person. That person writes another paragraph and hands it to the next person, and so on. This last method is sure to produce surprises, as well as laughs!

It's Really Something!

If you're still not sure that air is a physical substance and not just empty space, this activity will prove it.

What you need

Medium-sized glass jar
Funnel
Modeling clay
Water in a measuring cup
Food coloring (optional)
Pencil

What to do

1. Stick some clay around the top of the jar so that the narrow end of the funnel is held in place in the center. The bottom of the funnel should reach about 5 centimeters (2 inches) into the jar. Smooth out the clay, making sure that you have a tight seal with no holes.

2. Pour some water slowly into the funnel. You might want to color the water first with food coloring so that you can see it more clearly. What happens?

3. Now carefully stick the pencil through the clay down into the jar. What happens this time? Why?

Here's the story

At first the water stayed in the funnel because the jar was already full—of air. When you made a hole in the clay with the pencil, you let some air escape. Then the water could flow into the jar.

You're Full of Hot Air!

How much air can you blow out of your lungs in one breath? Try this activity to find out. You'll need a friend to help, so make it a contest. Careful—water can be very messy!

What you need

Large plastic pop bottle with top
Plastic tubing (buy this at a hardware or home supplies store)
A deep sink
A marker or grease pencil
Measuring cup

What to do

1. Fill the bottle with water and screw on the top. Half-fill the sink with water. Turn the bottle upside down in the sink so that the top is under the water. Now carefully remove the bottle cap. (The water will stay inside the bottle.)

2. Put one end of the tubing inside the bottle. Take as deep a breath as you can and blow into the other end of the tubing. Some of the water will come out into the sink. Ask your friend to mark the water level on the outside of the bottle.

3. Tip all the water out of the bottle and fill it to the mark your friend made. Now pour that water into the measuring cup. That's how much air you blew out. Now it's your friend's turn to try his or her lung power.

Sun Cooker

On a hot sunny day, you don't need a fire to have a cookout—all you need is the sun. That's right—the sun will actually cook hot dogs. Be sure to wear sunglasses and slather on lots of sunscreen when you try this, though. If the sun can cook hot dogs, it can also cook you! This is definitely a group activity, so call up your friends. And don't forget the buns, relish, and mustard!

What you need

Round cereal box with lid (one per kid)
Scissors
Aluminum foil
Hot dogs
Long forks or sharpened sticks

What to do

1. Cut a long window in the side of each cereal box. Line the inside of the box with foil, shiny side out.

2. Go outdoors and find a good sunny spot. (Remember the First Rule of the Sun: never look directly at it!) Aim the box so that the sun's rays hit the window. Now put a hot dog on the end of a fork or stick and hold it inside your "oven." In a while, it will start to cook.

3. It's chow time! Another reason to say thanks to the sun for its endless gift of solar power.

Fab Flowers

Plants can't move from place to place, but there's plenty of movement going on inside them. See it happen as you create these unearthly beauties.

What you need

3 glasses of water
Red, blue, and green food coloring
2 white flowers (such as chrysanthemums)
Scissors
A stalk of celery

What to do

1. Add a different color of food coloring to each glass of water.
2. Trim the ends of both flowers. Carefully cut up the middle of one flower stem to just under the flower head.
3. Put the flower with the whole stem into the green water. Put one half of the split stem into the red water and the other half into the blue water.
4. Trim the end off the celery so that it's not too long and put the stalk in the red water.
5. Put the three glasses in a warm place for two or three hours. Then have a look. What's happened?
6. Check the bottom of the celery stalk. What do you see? How did the coloring get from the water up to the tops of the flowers and celery leaves?

Here's the story

Plants—including trees—have tiny tubes that lead from the roots to every leaf, flower, and fruit. The tubes are the transportation system of the plant. Water, nutrients, gases, and sugars travel through these tubes to wherever they're needed in the plant. The red dots you saw in the celery stalk marked the ends of the tubes leading to the leaves. Can you figure out what happened in the flower with the split stem?

Space Creatures

Remember those invisible body creatures we talked about in Chapter 5? They're on you and in the air. They're all over your home and outside. In short, they're everywhere. Want to say hello to some of the unseen life-forms that share your space? Here's a way you can have a look without using a microscope. You'll need an adult to help with this, since you'll be using the stove and boiling water.

What you need

    4 empty jars with lids
    Measuring cup
    Saucepan
    One envelope of unflavored gelatin
    Spoon
    Marker
    Paper for labels
    Tape
    Scissors
    String

1. First sterilize your jars with boiling water. This will kill any life-forms that are already on them. Wash the jars and then pour boiling water into them. Pour boiling water over the lids too. You can do this in the sink. Then don't touch them until they're cool.

2. While the jars are cooling, measure 500 milliliters (2 cups) of very hot tap water into the saucepan. Pour the gelatin into the pan and stir until the gelatin is dissolved. (The liquid should be smooth, not gritty.) You may have to heat the gelatin a bit on the stove to dissolve it completely.

3. Pour 50 milliliters (¼ cup) of gelatin into one of the jars and screw the lid on tightly. Label it "control" and set it aside. You won't be putting anything into this jar. It's there to compare with the other jars. Then pour 50 milliliters (¼ cup) of gelatin into each of the other three jars.

4. Cut three pieces of string about 40 centimeters (15 inches) long. Put one of the pieces into the saucepan and leave it there for a minute or so, until the string is soaked with gelatin. Then drag the string across any surface you want to test for critters—a rug, your bedroom floor, a sofa or table. Put the string into a jar and screw on the lid. Label it "rug" or wherever you dragged the string. Do the same with the other two pieces of string. You might want to take a sample somewhere outdoors.

5. Now wait. It might take a few weeks for your beings to show up, but check every day. Use a magnifying glass if you have one. You won't see anything big, but you should see something, as your critters reproduce. Are there different kinds of beings in each jar? Do you see anything in the "control" jar?

Here's the story

Gelatin is food for life-forms. It lets them grow and multiply until you can see a pile-up of them. If the "control" jar was completely sterilized, you shouldn't see anything growing in it. It lets you know that whatever grows in the other three jars must have come from the strings and the places you dragged them.

Salmon Journal

Look again at the picture on page 69. You might want to take out a library book and learn more about the heroic Pacific salmon. Then imagine that you are a salmon. Write a journal describing your adventures at each stage of your voyage to the sea and back. Start with the day you were born in a river and end when you return there to spawn. Along the way, describe how you feel, what you see around you, what you eat, what other animals you meet. Being a salmon, you'll probably have to pull off some narrow escapes.

Be an Animal

If you want to learn about nature, the best way is to be part of it. Get a small group of friends and parents together. Pick a safe natural place—maybe a park, conservation area, or beach. Wear long pants, and don't forget the sunscreen and bug repellent. Fill a backpack with a mat to sit on, art materials, a journal and a pen, and a small gift for the animals, such as a few nuts or acorns. You might want to add a book for identifying birds or plants in your area.

When you get to the site, each person chooses a special spot to sit in. Then you sit and just watch. No talking or moving. If you want to move your head, move very slowly—no faster than the second hand on a watch. Look for larger and small animals, birds, and insects. Look carefully at the trees, flowers, and grass around you. Listen to the sounds. To hear better, give yourself deer ears— cup your palms behind your ears. You'll be able to hear very soft sounds. Smell the air—can you pick up any interesting smells?

The first time you try this, 10 minutes will probably be long enough. Then write in your journal about what you saw, heard, and felt. Did the experience call up any memories?

You might want to write a story from the point of view of an animal you saw. Draw a picture of whatever interests you, either the whole scene or detail, such as a leaf or an anthill. When you're ready to go, clean up your spot and leave your gift of thanks.

Diary of a Hunter-Gatherer

Imagine that you are a child growing up long, long ago. Write a diary entry describing a day or a week in your life. First read some books about an ancient culture that interests you so that you can tell as true a story as possible. Maybe you belong to a very early group of nomads, who hunt wild animals and pick grasses and berries for food. Or you might belong to a later culture, such as the Incas, Celts, or Vikings. Describe your home, clothes, food and daily activities. Perhaps record a conversation. You might want to add drawings to illustrate your diary.

INDEX

Page numbers in **bold** refer to illustrations or photographs.